Malcolm X

Militant Black Leader

Black Americans of Achievement

LEGACY EDITION

Muhammad Ali
Frederick Douglass
W.E.B. Du Bois
Marcus Garvey
Alex Haley
Langston Hughes
Jesse Jackson
Coretta Scott King
Martin Luther King, Jr.
Malcolm X
Thurgood Marshall
Jesse Owens
Rosa Parks
Colin Powell
Sojourner Truth
Harriet Tubman
Nat Turner
Booker T. Washington

Black Americans of Achievement

LEGACY EDITION

Malcolm X

Militant Black Leader

Jack Rummel

With additional text written by
Heather Lehr Wagner

Consulting Editor, Revised Edition
Heather Lehr Wagner

Senior Consulting Editor, First Edition
Nathan Irvin Huggins
Director, W.E.B. Du Bois Institute
for Afro-American Research
Harvard University

CHELSEA HOUSE
PUBLISHERS
An imprint of Infobase Publishing

Cover: Malcolm X prepares to speak to a group in New York in 1964.

Malcolm X: Militant Black Leader

Copyright © 2005 by Infobase Publishing

Chelsea House
An imprint of Infobase Publishing
132 West 31st Street
New York NY 10001

ISBN-10: 0-7910-8162-1
ISBN-13: 978-0-7910-8162-4

Library of Congress Cataloging-in-Publication Data

Rummel, Jack.
   Malcolm X : militant black leader / Jack Rummel, with additional text by Heather Lehr Wagner.—Rev. ed.
      p. cm.—(Black Americans of achievement)
   ISBN 0-7910-8162-1
   1. Black Muslims—Biography—Juvenile literature. 2. African Americans—Biography—Juvenile literature. I. Wagner, Heather Lehr. II. Title. III. Series.
BP223.Z8L577 2004
320.54'6'092—dc22   2004008454

Series and cover design by Keith Trego

Printed in the United States of America

Bang 21C 10 9 8 7 6 5 4 3

This book is printed on acid-free paper.

Contents

Introduction

Nearly 20 years ago Chelsea House Publishers began to publish the first volumes in the series called BLACK AMERICANS OF ACHIEVEMENT. This series eventually numbered over a hundred books and profiled outstanding African Americans from many walks of life. Today, if you ask school teachers and school librarians what comes to mind when you mention Chelsea House, many will say—"Black Americans of Achievement."

The mix of individuals whose lives we covered was eclectic, to say the least. Some were well known—Muhammad Ali and Dr. Martin Luther King, Jr, for example. But others, such as Harriet Tubman and Sojourner Truth, were lesser-known figures who were introduced to modern readers through these books. The individuals profiled were chosen for their actions, their deeds, and ultimately their influence on the lives of others and their impact on our nation as a whole. By sharing these stories of unique Americans, we hoped to illustrate how ordinary individuals can be transformed by extraordinary circumstances to become people of greatness. We also hoped that these special stories would encourage young-adult readers to make their own contribution to a better world. Judging from the many wonderful letters we have received about the BLACK AMERICANS OF ACHIEVEMENT biographies over the years from students, librarians, and teachers, they have certainly fulfilled the goal of inspiring others!

Now, some 20 years later, we are publishing 18 volumes of the original BLACK AMERICANS OF ACHIEVEMENT series in revised editions to bring the books into the twenty-first century and make them available to a new generation of young-adult readers. The selection was based on the importance of these figures to American life and the popularity of the original books with our readers. These revised editions have a new full-color design and, wherever possible, we have added color photographs. The books have new features, including quotes from the writings and speeches of leaders and interesting and unusual facts about their lives. The concluding section of each book gives new emphasis to the legacy of these men and women for the current generation of readers.

The lives of these African-American leaders are unique and remarkable. By transcending the barriers that racism placed in their paths, they are examples of the power and resiliency of the human spirit and are an inspiration to readers.

We present these wonderful books to our audience for their reading pleasure.

Lee M. Marcott
Chelsea House Publishers
August 2004

The Cities Are Burning

On the afternoon of May 21, 1964, nearly 60 newspaper reporters crowded into the VIP lounge at Kennedy International Airport on the outskirts of New York City, anxiously awaiting the arrival of militant black leader Malcolm X. The journalists, most of whom were white and worked for the major New York newspapers, were worried about their approaching deadlines. Yet all of the reporters preferred to risk being late with their copy than leave without hearing what Malcolm X had to say upon his return from a tour of Africa and the Middle East.

The 39-year-old civil rights activist had been away from the United States for only five weeks, but during his brief absence racial relations had become even more strained. Many blacks were voicing their anger over how little progress had been made on the issue of civil rights. Many whites strongly opposed the few social reforms that were instituted to bring about greater racial equality.

Police and local black leaders had predicted that mounting racial tensions would lead to a summer of violence in the black ghettos of several major American cities. Nowhere did this threat of violence loom greater than in New York, which boasted the largest black population in the nation. In fact, the city's police department had recently claimed to have uncovered a black vigilante group, the "Blood Brothers," that had been posing as a gun club. Their aim, according to the police, was to spill blood and incite violence.

Many people, including those in the media, were searching for clues as to what would happen next, and Malcolm X was thought to be an important resource. Noted for his willingness to approach controversial subjects that more moderate civil rights leaders usually avoided, he had gained the trust of America's urban blacks. He was not a man to mince words, and he was not afraid to hammer away with his demands for changes in American society.

Malcolm X's ultimate goal was the liberation of black Americans from what he believed was a brutally oppressive, white-dominated power structure. While less revolutionary black leaders, especially the Reverend Martin Luther King, Jr., struggled to bring about greater racial integration in American society, Malcolm X repeatedly stated that the old order must be completely destroyed and replaced with new political and economic systems that allow blacks and whites to share power equally. Knowing how unlikely it was that the old structures would collapse, he often called upon black Americans to cut their ties with their country and found a separate nation. Yet as his flight from Algeria touched down at the airport, he was returning to a country that was still far from ready to accept his radical programs.

When Malcolm X emerged from the international arrivals gate, he was greeted by his wife and children and a group of his close associates. There was a sudden, excited bustling in the lounge area as the reporters caught sight of the tall, lean man with a wispy new beard. They flocked around him and unleashed a barrage of questions.

Race riots broke out in New York City during the summer of 1964 after a student was shot and killed by police in Harlem. Here, officers on horses confront a group of men during the disturbances.

Only after Malcolm X seated himself at a nearby table and faced the reporters would he allow himself to be interviewed. He had become a master at using the media to publicize his political message, treating press sessions like a kind of game. The game was a serious one, though, for its object was the creation of a black political revolution in the United States.

The first question posed to Malcolm X was about the Blood Brothers, to whom he supposedly had ties. Indeed, he was the first black leader to have made a public statement calling for blacks to form gun clubs to protect themselves. If Malcolm X supported the Blood Brothers, one reporter asked, was he not "a teacher, a fomentor of violence?"

Malcolm X answered by pointing out what he believed were contradictions in the way the press—mainly the white press—

wrote about the issue of self-defense in the case of racial attacks. It was considered normal for whites to buy guns for their self-defense, he said, but when blacks took up arms to protect themselves against lynch mobs, it was viewed as a potentially dangerous situation. "I'm for justice," he told the reporters. "When the law fails to protect Negroes from whites' attacks, then those Negroes should use arms, if necessary, to defend themselves."

Another reporter wanted to know why Malcolm X always had to "stir up" blacks. It was a question that seemed almost ludicrous to Malcolm X, who spent most of his life among people whose poverty and misery had gone virtually unnoticed by much of white America. He wearily answered, "It takes no one to stir up the sociological dynamite that stems from unemployment, bad housing, and inferior education already in the ghettos. This explosively criminal condition has existed for so long it needs no fuse; it fuses itself."

Few of the reporters seemed to notice during the interview that Malcolm X had undergone a dramatic transformation in his thinking. He had initially become a public figure as a clergyman of the Nation of Islam, a black religious movement based largely on the teachings of Muhammad, the seventh-century founder of the religion of Islam. Like most followers of the Nation of Islam (who are known as Black Muslims), he had learned to view all whites as "devils" and had indicated his allegiance to the Nation by changing his name from Malcolm Little to Malcolm X. (For many Black Muslims, bold-looking letter Xs are used to replace the surnames given to their ancestors by slave owners.)

Malcolm X, however, had recently separated from the movement and altered his views on America's racial problems. While in the Middle East, he saw Muslims of many different races sharing a common bond of friendship. Deeply affected by what he witnessed on his travels, he told the press, "I have become convinced that some whites do want to help cure the rampant racism which is on the path to destroying this country."

Malcolm X left the interview knowing that despite having spoken of the urgent need for an improvement in race relations, the headlines in the morning papers would most likely proclaim: MALCOLM X ADVOCATES ARMED NEGROES! He had already grown accustomed to having inaccurate stories printed about him. So long as he urged blacks to resist racial oppression "by any means necessary," he would continue to carry with him a reputation as the one person who could either start or stop a race riot. "I don't know if I could start one," he said, but "I don't know if I'd want to stop one." It is not that he hoped to see a wave of destructive violence sweep through America, but he believed something must be done to jolt his countrymen into understanding that the black ghettos were filled with a terrible sense of desperation.

As feared, riots broke out in New York later in the summer—a single incident was all that was needed to set off a neighborhood already seething with frustration and hatred for an overbearing police force that acted more like an occupying army than an agency of justice. A 15-year-old student in the black district of Harlem was shot and killed by a police officer on July 16, 1964. For the next week, the streets of Harlem and

IN HIS OWN WORDS...

Malcolm X believed that more fundamental rights needed to be achieved before the civil rights movement could accomplish anything of note. In "Racism: the Cancer that is Destroying America," published in the *Egyptian Gazette* on August 25, 1964, he wrote:

> The common goal of 22 million Afro-Americans is respect as human beings, the God-given right to be a human being. Our common goal is to obtain the human rights that America has been denying us. We can never get civil rights in America until our human rights are first restored. We will never be recognized as citizens there until we are first recognized as humans.

the Bedford-Stuyvesant section of Brooklyn became a battle zone filled with gunfire and flaming buildings. The cities had begun to burn, and the fury felt by blacks in the ghettos would soon cause many more cities to be set ablaze.

This was Malcolm X's world—a violent world, seething with tension, like a time bomb about to explode. Once the fuse was lit, the changes he had been longing for seemed close at hand.

2

The Outsider

Malcolm X was born on May 19, 1925, in Omaha, Nebraska. The fourth of Earl and Louise Little's eight children, Malcolm Little (as he was then called) entered a world full of violence and fear. Only a few weeks before his birth, the dreaded night riders of the Ku Klux Klan, the most notorious white supremacist group in America, paid a visit to his family. The Klan's terrorist attack—part of its campaign to intimidate anyone who was not white and Anglo-Saxon—was the first in a series of grim incidents that devastated Malcolm's family during his early life.

Malcolm's father, Earl, was a strong-willed and outspoken Baptist minister who happened to be preaching in another community on the night when a band of white-robed horsemen appeared at his home. Waving torches and rifles, the Klan members surrounded the house and called for the Reverend Earl Little to step outside. They planned on lynching him in full view of his family.

Malcolm's visibly pregnant mother, Louise, was alone in the house with her three children: Wilfred, Philbert, and Hilda. Although terrified by the ring of fire formed by the horsemen outside her home, she walked out on the porch and told the Klansmen her husband was away on business. Disappointed, they smashed the windows of the house with their rifle butts and warned her that her husband had better leave town.

Earl Little was not the sort of person who bowed before anyone because of intimidation. Born in Reynolds, Georgia, he had grown up in the South in an atmosphere of racial violence. Three of his brothers had been killed by whites.

The attacks were part of the bloody drama staged throughout much of the South after the Civil War. Constitutional amendments had granted citizenship and the right to vote to blacks in 1868 and 1870, but Southern whites were determined to deny them these privileges. Through racially discriminatory "Jim Crow" laws established by state legislatures, they prohibited blacks from using the same facilities—including schools, hospitals, theaters, and railroad cars—as whites. Those who protested against the unfair system of racial segregation were often beaten. A great many others were lynched. (For additional information on this topic, enter "Jim Crow laws" into any search engine and browse the sites listed.)

Malcolm's father took up preaching because it enabled him to speak out for black rights under the protection of the church. After being ordained as a Baptist minister, he moved to Philadelphia, Pennsylvania. There he married and had three children with a woman whom he subsequently divorced. He then married Louise and started a new family.

A restless man who was given to wandering from place to place, Earl Little moved with Louise and his growing family to Omaha, where he started a small farm to supplement the earnings he made as a minister. He also became an activist for Marcus Garvey's Universal Negro Improvement Association (UNIA), a militant organization that urged blacks to stop trying to integrate themselves into white society; the UNIA maintained that they should leave America instead and establish an independent black nation in Africa as part of a

Marcus Garvey

Malcolm X's father, Earl Little, was an activist for Marcus Garvey's Universal Negro Improvement Association (UNIA). Young Malcolm attended UNIA meetings with his father and was impressed by the organization's militant stance and Garvey's colorful uniforms.

Marcus Garvey was born in Jamaica on August 17, 1887. He attended school for seven years before becoming a printer and quickly joined the printers' union. At the age of 20, he was elected vice president of the compositors' branch of the printers' union and helped lead a strike before the union dissolved.

In 1911, Garvey moved to England. While studying at Birbeck College, he met blacks from British colonies who were working to achieve their countries' independence. Impressed by their commitment, Garvey returned to Jamaica determined to better the status of his people. He established the UNIA there, and by 1916 had traveled to the United States to organize American branches of his new organization. Its message—urging action against lynching, Jim Crow laws, and racial discrimination—was very popular among blacks. By 1919, the UNIA had more than two million members and 30 branches.

Garvey soon adopted the stance that American whites would never agree to end discrimination and treat blacks as equals. He began to advocate the creation of a separate, independent nation in Africa where all blacks would live. He suggested arming a military unit to seize African territory from any whites who had settled there, and, in a highly controversial move, met with members of the Ku Klux Klan to discuss the planned relocation of all blacks to Africa.

Garvey formed a navigation and trading company and urged his black supporters to invest in it. Financial irregularities plagued the company, however, and Garvey was arrested and charged with fraud. He served half of his five-year prison sentence before being deported to Jamaica.

Garvey attempted to win a seat in Jamaica's colonial legislature but lost the election. He lectured throughout Europe and Canada and eventually moved to England. He died in London in 1940. Ironically, despite his calls for a "Back to Africa" movement, Africa remained one continent that the well-traveled activist never visited.

"Back to Africa" movement. It was largely because of his position as a spokesman for this black nationalist movement that Malcolm's father was targeted by the Klan.

A MOVE TO MICHIGAN

Shortly after the Klan's attack—and Malcolm's birth—the Littles joined many other black families who left their farms in the South and Midwest and moved to industrial centers in the North, where there seemed to be greater economic opportunities. Malcolm's family stayed briefly in Milwaukee, Wisconsin. Then they settled in Lansing, Michigan, where his father planned to run a store while continuing his preaching.

At first, Lansing seemed to be a place where the family could put down roots. In this Northern town—far from the violent racism he had experienced elsewhere—Earl Little felt he could establish a strong black rights organization. He soon discovered, however, that the ugly specter of racial oppression that had haunted him in the South was also present in the North.

When Malcolm was four years old, night riders again attacked his family. A local group of white supremacists, wearing black robes and calling themselves the Black Legion, had become aware of Earl Little's efforts to organize the black community and had decided to stop him. This time, instead of surrounding his house on horseback, the night riders crept up and set fire to his home.

Malcolm's father ran outside with a pistol and fired at the men after yelling a warning to his family. As flames engulfed their home, Malcolm and his siblings scrambled through the doorway; their mother escaped with the baby, Yvonne, just seconds before the walls caved in. It was a nightmarish scene that became vividly implanted in Malcolm's memory.

The Littles failed to receive any assistance from the police, who were more interested in Earl Little's gun than his attackers. In fact, after the Littles settled in a new home in the nearby town of East Lansing, the police raided the house on several occasions in search of the pistol. The gun, hidden in a pillowcase, was never discovered.

Life in East Lansing was just as unpleasant for the Littles as it had been in Lansing. East Lansing had a curfew forbidding blacks to be outdoors after sundown; the ordinance was too much for the Littles to tolerate. They moved to a four-room house built by Malcolm's father on a plot of land a few miles outside of town. Their new home included a garden and a pen for chickens and turkeys.

The modest farm helped the Littles cope with the ravaging effects of the Great Depression, which occurred after the New York Stock Exchange crashed in the fall of 1929. Industrial centers in the North—including the automobile factories around Lansing—were especially hard hit by the failing economy, and the area's blacks were the hardest hit of all. White workers, victims of soaring unemployment, started to seize the low-paying jobs previously held only by blacks.

Courting the area's dissatisfied blacks, Earl Little continued to hold secret meetings for members of Garvey's Universal Negro Improvement Association. Malcolm, who sometimes accompanied his father to these meetings, was impressed by a picture he saw of Garvey; the founder of the UNIA was garbed in an ornate uniform complete with a plumed hat. The young boy was equally thrilled by an anthem sung at the meetings: "Up, You Mighty Race." The lyrics, which told Garvey's followers, "You can accomplish what you will!," filled Malcolm with confidence that times would improve.

This sense of optimism did not last for long. One day in 1931, after he had engaged in a loud argument with his wife, Earl Little stormed out of the house and was not seen for several hours. He was later found on a section of trolley tracks in downtown East Lansing. One side of his head had been beaten in, and a trolley car had run over him, cutting him almost in half. Astonishingly, he clung to life for more

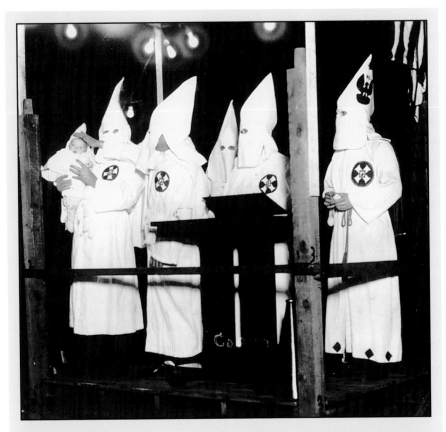

From his birth, Malcolm X lived in a world of racism and violence.
Malcolm's father was a Baptist minister who was targeted by the Ku Klux
Klan (seen here), and possibly killed by members of a white supremacist
group in Michigan.

than two hours before he died. His family and friends were
sure that members of the Black Legion had attacked him and
left him on the tracks to die, although his murderers were
never found.

The night riders, it seemed, had finally destroyed Earl Little.
Yet the preacher from Georgia left a militant legacy to those
who had listened to his calls for black unity. Among them was
his six-year-old son Malcolm, who already knew more than
any child should know about death and violence.

STRUGGLING FOR SURVIVAL

The death of Earl Little left his family in dire straits. For a year, Louise Little was able to provide for the family after receiving payments from one of two life insurance policies her husband had taken out on himself. The second insurance company refused to make any payments, claiming that Earl Little had committed suicide. Louise Little protested that the ruling was ridiculous, but she never received the money owed her.

Left without its chief provider during the worst years of the depression, Malcolm's family struggled to survive. His oldest brother, Wilfred, dropped out of school and took on any small jobs he could find. Having always been a housewife, Louise Little was unprepared for the burden of supporting eight children by herself (Yvonne, Reginald, Wesley, and Robert were born after Malcolm). She had to leave her children in the care of her oldest daughter, Hilda, while she looked for work. At times, Louise was able to find jobs as a seamstress or maid in the homes of East Lansing's white families, who assumed because of her light skin that she was white. When her prejudiced employers discovered that she was black, she was usually fired on the spot.

The Littles often had no more to eat than a bowl of corn-meal or dandelion greens. Yet they managed to scrape by with some help from friends and neighbors. After Louise Little became a member of the Seventh Day Adventists, one of the few religious groups that ignored America's color line, the family dinner table began to include items contributed by other congregation members. Because the Adventists were opposed to eating pork, however, Louise had to refuse some of the donations of sympathetic neighbors. Malcolm and his brother Philbert contributed by hunting for rabbits and bullfrogs, which they sold to white families.

An energetic and restless boy with a light, coppery complexion and dark reddish hair that set him apart from his darker-skinned siblings, Malcolm often fought with his brothers. At the local school, however, where he and the other Little children were the only black students, they banded together to defend themselves against white classmates. From a young age, Malcolm learned to harden himself against the racial slurs that other students used in his presence.

For a short while, it appeared that the Littles might be able to survive as a family: Louise met a man who seemed interested in marrying her. When he stopped visiting her, perhaps overwhelmed by the thought of becoming a stepfather to eight children, she sank into a state of listlessness and took little notice of what was going on around her. She found it impossible to take on steady work, and she was forced to apply to the state welfare department for financial assistance.

The intrusion of state welfare agents into their lives was a demoralizing blow to the family. The welfare agents asked the children why Malcolm's skin color was so much lighter than his brothers' and sisters' and why their mother refused to let them eat pork when they were starving. Such questions confused the children and created tensions and divisions within the family.

By the time Malcolm was 10, he began to stay away from home, where he was continually reminded of his family's poverty. He spent most evenings at the home of the Gohannases, a black couple who were raising a nephew about Malcolm's age. He also spent time with a group of young men (both black and white) who sometimes met at night to engage in such pranks as pushing over outhouses on nearby farms.

Malcolm soon turned to more criminal acts. He drifted up and down the streets of Lansing during the afternoons, stealing candy, fruit, and other items from stores. He was caught many times, until finally the local court authorities decided that Louise could no longer control Malcolm. They determined to put him in someone else's charge, in part so he would not be a bad influence on his brothers and sisters. Malcolm was relieved when the Gohannases volunteered to take him into their household, for the tensions at his own home had become unbearable.

In 1937, shortly after Malcolm was separated from his family, the state welfare department committed his mother to a mental hospital, where she was to remain for the next 26 years. The Little children became wards of the state, and most of them were sent to live with families in the area. Only Wilfred and Hilda, who were by then old enough to be on their own, were allowed to stay in the Little house.

Malcolm's bitter feelings toward the state authorities, whom he blamed for destroying his family, sometimes boiled over, especially when he was in school. Although he was a very intelligent young man and usually earned good grades, he frequently disrupted the classroom. Finally, he was expelled from school and placed in a juvenile detention center in Mason, Michigan, a town about 20 miles from Lansing, before being sent on to reform school.

The change in Malcolm's surroundings seemed to calm him down a little. Like all but the most violent children at the detention center, he had his own room and ate his meals with the facility's directors, a white couple whose last name was the Swerlin. Malcolm could be quite charming when he wanted to be, and the Swerlins took an immediate liking to their newest ward and appreciated his eagerness to help with the center's chores.

When the time came for Malcolm to be sent to a reform school, the Swerlins asked him if he wanted to stay with them while he finished his education. He readily agreed to their proposal and was enrolled in Mason's junior high school, whose student body was predominantly white. This time at school, however, his behavior was much improved, and so were his grades: He ranked third in his class academically. He became so popular with the other students that at the end of his first year at Mason, he was elected vice-president of his class.

On the surface, Malcolm seemed to be getting along well with the Swerlins and his classmates. Underneath, though, he was deeply troubled by their attitude toward him and other blacks. The Swerlins used derogatory terms to refer to blacks without realizing the impact of their words on Malcolm. He was popular among the students, he thought, only because they found him strange and exotic, not because they really liked him or cared about his feelings. As he would write later in *The Autobiography of Malcolm X*, "Even though [whites] appeared to open the door, it was still closed." The white world did not want to accept him as an equal.

A NEW LIFE

In the spring of 1939, Malcolm received a letter from his half-sister Ella, a child from his father's first marriage. She had become a successful businesswoman and community leader in Boston, Massachusetts. She was also known to be generous in helping her relatives. Having heard what had befallen her father's second family, she had written to Malcolm and his siblings to find out if she could visit them later in the year to see if she could help them, too.

During her visit with the Littles, Ella discovered that she and Malcolm shared many characteristics, including an enthusiastic approach to life. She invited him to spend the following summer with her in Boston. It was an invitation he was quick to accept.

When Malcolm arrived in Boston, he discovered that Ella lived in the wealthiest part of Roxbury, one of the predominantly black sections of the city. There he was able to experience for the first time in his life what it was like to be a privileged black. He listened to the articulate discussions of Ella's socialite friends, admired the sharply dressed young men and women, and delighted in the city's lively jazz scene. The bands of such top musicians as Duke Ellington and Count Basie came to Boston and played in packed ballrooms on Friday and Saturday nights.

In 1940, Malcolm moved to this house in Boston to live with his half-sister, Ella. He was fascinated by the activity and fast-paced nature of the city, and hoped it would provide him with excitement and opportunities.

Fourteen-year-old Malcolm was also a little intimidated by Boston: The pace of life was faster than anything he had ever experienced. Yet big-city life fascinated him, and he quickly felt at home there. He regretted having to return to Michigan when the summer came to an end.

Back in Mason, Malcolm could not stop thinking about Boston. Life in a small town seemed much too limited. When one of his favorite teachers advised him to give up his ambition of becoming a lawyer because there was no place in society for black attorneys, Malcolm gave up on his schoolwork and wrote to Ella, asking if she could arrange for him to move in with her. He was elated when he heard she had secured the agreement of the Michigan state welfare department for his change of residence.

In May 1940, soon after his 15th birthday, Malcolm boarded a bus for the lengthy ride to Boston. Yet the trip went by quickly. The excitement and promise of the city's lights kept spinning around in his imagination. A new world was waiting for him, and he was too inexperienced to know the dangers that lay in wait for him in the city.

3

Detroit Red's Streets

Malcolm arrived at Ella's house in the spring of 1940 a mixture of confidence and confusion: Although he looked and acted much older than his 15 years, he was still a tall and skinny teenager whose wrists and ankles jutted out of his light green suit. He immediately made it clear to Ella that he wanted to work rather than go to school. In that case, she told him, he should explore Boston before he found a job; he might never again have a chance to enjoy the city. Except for Ella, though, he had no one to show him around his new hometown.

Malcolm soon found his guide. One day, when he was hanging around a Roxbury pool hall, he met a young man named Shorty who had come to Boston many years before from Lansing, Michigan. Shorty took Malcolm under his wing and helped him find his first job: working as a shoe shiner at the Roseland State Ballroom, one of city's most popular music and dance halls.

Ella was not happy when she heard about Malcolm's new job. As a member of Boston's black elite, she wanted him to find work that was a bit more prestigious. Yet Malcolm had become disenchanted with black high society and believed that many of its members were either snobs, who put on airs, or hypocrites, who would say they were "in banking" when they were only janitors at a bank. Worst of all in his eyes, they were trying to imitate white society.

Malcolm was far more attracted to Roxbury's sporting life than to its black upper class. At his job at Roseland, he was not only among people with whom he felt more comfortable, but he also got to listen to some of the best jazz bands in the country. Like the other black employees in the dance hall, he held a somewhat privileged position, for only white customers were admitted to most shows; the Roseland management opened the hall to blacks just once or twice a month. In 1940, racial segregation was still being practiced in America, even in supposedly liberal Northern cities such as Boston.

Malcolm made money at Roseland by blacking shoes and also earned tips by bringing towels to rest room patrons. He quickly learned he could earn a larger tip than usual by loudly snapping the shoeshine cloth after finishing a job. He learned, too, that white customers liked to have blacks, such as Malcolm, defer to them, and they would pay him better if he bowed his head and acted submissive.

Yet Malcolm did not always act so innocently at Roseland. He supplemented his earnings by selling marijuana to some of the customers and by letting them know how to get in touch with the local prostitutes. He had few reservations about dealing in these kinds of illegal activities. They seemed acceptable ways of making a living because, he believed, he had little chance at being offered a reputable and well-paying job.

As he became more involved in Roxbury's world of drugs, drinking, and gambling, Malcolm developed an appetite for these vices as well. The more money he had to spend,

Although Malcolm was drawn in by the excitement of the vices and nightlife on the streets of Boston, he wanted to see the world, and soon moved to the almost entirely black neighborhood of Harlem in New York City. In Harlem, he spent his nights at bars and dance halls, like the famous Apollo Theater seen here, and earned a living through hustling.

the more he indulged. He also became hooked on dancing, especially a wild dance called the Lindy Hop. Named after Charles Lindbergh, the first aviator to pilot a plane across the Atlantic Ocean, the dance imitated an airplane taking off and landing as female dancers were thrown into the air and caught by their partners.

To go with his new lifestyle, Malcolm invested in a new wardrobe. He replaced his ill-fitting green suit with a sky-blue zoot suit, which featured baggy pants and a long, tight-waisted coat, and he added to it a blue felt hat and a gold pocketwatch chain that hung to his knees. He completed his new look by having his red hair "conked," or straightened: Conks were popular among young blacks in the ghetto, even though the lye used to straighten their hair also burned their scalp.

Later in his life, Malcolm viewed his conk hairstyle as "my first really big step toward self-degradation"—an act that symbolized his rejection of his black features and indicated his desire to appear more white. At the time, he looked on himself as being what was then known in the ghettos as a "hip cat." He was set on using his good looks and smart appearance to get what he wanted: money, women, and excitement.

Malcolm eventually quit his shoeshine job at Roseland because it interfered with his desire to be out on Roxbury's streets at night. He worked for a while as a soda fountain clerk at a drugstore near Ella's house. There, much to his half sister's delight, he met a proper young woman named Laura, whom he began taking to dances.

Malcolm and Laura had not been dating for very long, however, before he met a white woman named Sophia at a Roseland dance contest. Fascinated by the cool, sophisticated Sophia, Malcolm ended his relationship with Laura and began spending his nights hopping from barroom to barroom with Sophia. He was deaf to Ella's protests about his activities because his white girlfriend represented for him a glamorous new life. He was intoxicated with the world and grew impatient to see as much of it as he could. High on his list of places to visit was Harlem, the New York City district that boasted the largest black population in the country.

HARLEM BLUES

In December 1941, after the United States entered World War II, Malcolm finally found the opportunity to go to Harlem. Not only was the economy picking up, but job openings throughout the country were becoming plentiful because so many men were enlisting in the army. Malcolm, by lying about his age, was able to get a job selling sandwiches on the Yankee Clipper passenger train, which made daily runs between Boston and New York.

The 16-year-old hip cat was as awed by New York as he had been amazed by Boston a year and a half earlier. He was especially overwhelmed by Harlem, which in the early 1900s had become the leading center of black American culture and politics. During his first trip there, which included a visit to a popular nightclub called Small's Paradise, he gawked at the sheer number of people bustling around him, almost all of whom were black. It was as if Harlem were a whole city of black people, a world where racial prejudice was hidden away in the background. "I was mesmerized," he said later. "This world was where I belonged. On that night I had started on my way to becoming a Harlemite."

Malcolm moved out of Ella's house after he began working on the Yankee Clipper and rented a room in a Harlem boardinghouse. He attended the shows of such musical performers as Dizzy Gillespie and Billie Holiday on his days off from work. In Harlem's entertainment district, he befriended musicians who played at such noted dance halls as the Apollo Theater and the Savoy Ballroom.

No longer under Ella's watchful eye, Malcolm behaved more wildly in New York than he had in Boston. He dyed his hair bright red, stayed high on marijuana, and acted outrageously on the Yankee Clipper, racing up and down the train in the belief that his customers would give him larger tips if he entertained them. Yet he often crossed the line between entertainment and insult. Passengers filed complaints against him, and although he was warned to stop using profane language, he continued to act out of control. Finally, he was fired. At age 17, he was, he would later admit, "an uncouth, wild young Negro. I was really a clown, but my ignorance made me think I was sharp."

Malcolm found a job waiting tables in his favorite hangout, Small's Paradise, after he was fired by the railroad. While working there, he listened with fascination to the stories of the notorious Harlem underworld figures who gathered at the club. These men, who included the old pickpocket Fewclothes, the gambling racketeer West Indian Archie, and a group of garment-district mobsters known as the Forty Thieves, were veterans of the streets. They knew all the tricks of hustling: how to make damaged merchandise seem like valuable goods, where to hide drugs so the police could not find them, how to persuade gambling clients to pay their debts. They were quite willing to share their secrets with Malcolm. In fact, one of the Forty Thieves gave Malcolm an expensive new suit, a sign of acceptance into their ranks.

Malcolm's entry into the Harlem underworld was not accompanied by any fears that he was making a wrong decision. He did not believe he could make a living at a more respectable occupation. He also realized that hustling was a desperate gamble and enriched few who tried it. "Everybody in Harlem needed some kind of hustle to survive," he said, "and needed to stay high in some way to forget what they had to do to survive."

For the most part, Malcolm was careful not to risk his job at Small's by hustling at the club. One day, however, he told a lonely looking soldier where he could find a prostitute. The "soldier" was actually a police informant, and Malcolm was fired from the club.

Although Malcolm regretted losing his position, he decided not to take another legitimate job. He cared little about moral questions or the consequences of his actions. He saw himself as a smart, cynical loner. The key to success in life, he felt, was to use other people more than they used him. "A man," he believed, "should do anything that he was slick enough, or bad and bold enough, to do."

Malcolm wanted to become a full-time hustler, and for advice on how to succeed in hustling he turned to Sammy the Pimp, a friend who lived in the same boardinghouse. After Sammy advised him to start dealing drugs on the street, Malcolm plied his new trade energetically, selling marijuana to his musician friends. Older hustlers noted his successful business and decided to give him a nickname that would distinguish him as an underworld operator. Because he had grown up in Michigan and had a dyed conk, they soon began calling him Detroit Red.

Malcolm's drug dealing brought him some money at the beginning, until the police took notice of his activities. They began to follow him on the streets, sometimes stopping him and frisking him. He was never caught carrying any illegal drugs, having learned ways to quickly conceal marijuana packets whenever he saw a policeman approach.

One evening, however, Malcolm came home and discovered his apartment had been searched while he was out. He never kept his drugs at home, but he believed that the police had planted a concealed packet somewhere. Afraid they would soon raid his apartment, he decided to leave. For the next year, he was constantly on the move from one rooming house to the next, always fearful of a knock on the door.

LIFE OF CRIME

When Malcolm turned 18 in May 1943, he became eligible to be drafted into the army. Ordered to appear before his local draft board, he arrived at the induction center in his most outrageous zoot suit, determined to be disqualified from military service. While being examined by an army psychiatrist, he kept up a rapid, nonsensical banter that he stopped only so he could leap out of his chair and look under closet doors for intruders. Then he claimed he was planning to organize a bloody revolt of black soldiers against whites at army bases in the South. The shocked psychiatrist dropped his pencil. Malcolm was subsequently declared psychologically unfit for the army.

Malcolm's exaggerated behavior at the army induction center was only a show, but his real emotional condition was actually becoming frayed. His constant movement to new living quarters and his anxiety about being arrested had begun to make him feel like a hunted animal. His regular market among Harlem musicians had been closed off because of police surveillance, and he was forced to sell drugs to addicts in the most depressed parts of Harlem. His new customers were a desperate and dangerous group, and Malcolm said that in going into the worst ghetto areas, "You enter a world of animals and vultures. It becomes truly the survival of only the fittest."

Detroit Red thrashed around while trying to find a more lucrative hustle, but he was slowly being dragged down by his own game. Hounded so closely by the police that he was shut out from selling drugs in Harlem, he turned in desperation to armed robbery. After buying some guns, he traveled to towns outside New York and held up people on the streets. He soon found he had to be under the influence of cocaine or some other narcotic to be able to perform a robbery, and his heavy use of drugs hastened his downward slide.

By 1943, Malcolm was living in constant fear not only of the police but also of Harlem's underworld kingpins. On at least one occasion, he was roughed up by mobsters who suspected him of robbing one of their businesses. He lived with an arsenal of pistols, and tucking his compact .25 automatic "streetwear" into his waistband before leaving his apartment became as natural a habit as tying his shoelaces in the morning. "Full-time hustlers never can relax to appraise what they are doing and where they are bound," he later said. "If he ever relaxes, if he ever slows down, the other hungry restless foxes, ferrets, wolves, and vultures out there with him won't hesitate to make him their prey."

Economic conditions in Harlem, which were severe during the Great Depression, continued to deteriorate during World War II, and hustlers were driven into trying ever more dangerous ways to make money. While attempting to break into a heavily protected building, Malcolm and his friend Sammy were surprised by security guards and were fired upon. Both men escaped, but Sammy was slightly wounded.

After the aborted robbery, the security guards' description of Malcolm was posted on "Wanted" notices around Harlem. He decided to give up robbery and find a new occupation, but the only activities on which he seemed to be able to focus his attention were dreaming up new hustles, gambling, and taking narcotics.

CURRENT OF DISCONTENT

As Malcolm was facing an increasingly bleak future, racial tensions in Harlem were growing. Harlemites, like other black Americans, were incensed that blacks who enlisted in the army were forced to serve in segregated units and were given almost no opportunity to become officers. During a period when Americans were being asked to make sacrifices to help the war effort against Germany and Japan, many blacks were being lynched in the South, harassed in Northern ghettos, and excluded from well-paying jobs in the defense industry.

In Harlem, a rising young politician and preacher named Adam Clayton Powell, Jr., organized boycotts against utility companies and white-owned local businesses that practiced racial discrimination. Only limited steps were taken to correct the grievances, however, and an angry current of discontent continued to run through Harlem. Finally, in August 1943, the district erupted after a black soldier was shot by a white policeman in a Harlem hotel. Black mobs roamed the district's streets, smashing the windows of the area's mainly white-owned businesses and looting the stores.

Adam Clayton Powell, Jr.

While Malcolm X was dealing drugs and committing armed robbery, another young black man in Harlem was organizing boycotts against utility companies and other white-owned businesses that practiced racial discrimination. This determined politician and preacher was Adam Clayton Powell, Jr.

Powell was born on November 29, 1908, in New Haven, Connecticut. As a young boy, he moved with his family to New York City, where his father began developing the Abyssinian Baptist Church. He graduated from Colgate University and then received his Master of Arts in religious education from Columbia University. When the Depression ravaged Harlem and the rest of the United States, Powell worked at his father's church, but his focus quickly shifted to the civil rights movement.

Determined to correct the discrimination and poverty crippling the black community, Powell organized rent strikes and boycotts of restaurants, stores, bus lines, telephone companies, and even Harlem Hospital, urging them to hire and promote black employees. From 1936 to 1944, he published *The Peoples Voice*, a newspaper that publicized his efforts to correct injustice and discrimination. In 1945, he was elected to Congress, where he quickly ensured that the informal regulations reserving capitol facilities for white congressional members only were changed.

Throughout his congressional career, Powell clashed with segregationists and worked to ensure that nearly every piece of legislation carried an antidiscrimination rider. His committee work included important measures to approve minimum wage increases, education and training for the deaf, and federal support for student loans and school lunches.

Accused of slander, Powell was investigated by the Judiciary Committee and stripped of his committee chairmanship in 1967. Two years later, a ruling in his favor restored his seat in Congress. He unsuccessfully sought reelection in 1970 before retiring. He died in 1972.

Thousands of police were called in to quell the riot with a show of force, but blacks fought back, sometimes with rifles and pistols. Before the violence ended, 5 people were dead, more than 400 were injured, and Harlem's business district lay in ruins. Along with many other Harlemites, Malcolm saw the 1943 riot as a gesture of black defiance not only against the white politicians and businessmen who controlled New York City but against a police force regularly accused of assaults on blacks.

Although there were several reasons for the unrest, the riot had a single effect on Harlem: The community was devastated. Whites stopped coming to the area, and its once glittering theater district went out of business. The black community became poorer and more isolated than it had ever been before, and unemployment soared.

Malcolm survived by becoming a numbers runner, one of the people who collect tickets for the illegal lottery game controlled by mobsters. Two close scrapes almost cost him his life. First, a mob family suspected him of having robbed one of its dice games, and it sent two gunmen to kill him. Malcolm was inside a phone booth when the mob's executioners found him, and they told him to step outside so that they "could hold court." The verdict had already been given, but fortunately for the accused a policeman suddenly appeared and he was able to walk away.

Malcolm was still in shock from this incident when one of his underworld friends, West Indian Archie, accused him of cheating on a bet. He was told to return the money he had won or suffer the consequences. Only a small amount of money was involved, but each man was determined to protect his reputation. "A hustler could never afford to have it demonstrated that he could be bluffed, that he could be frightened by a threat, that he lacked nerve," Malcolm later said of this incident. The two men finally had a showdown in a Harlem bar, but friends stopped them before it turned into a shoot-out.

Racial tensions were brewing in Harlem, and in August of 1943 the tension erupted into violence after a black soldier was shot by a white policeman. During one night of rioting, six blacks were killed and hundreds more were injured and arrested. Here, police patrol a Harlem street to prevent further violence.

Malcolm was walking down a Harlem street two days later when a car pulled up beside him. Instinctively, he pulled out his gun, but stopped and breathed a sigh of relief when he realized that the driver was Shorty, his friend from Boston. He had heard about Malcolm's troubles and had driven to New York to help him out. Six hours later, the two were back in Roxbury.

Malcolm's escape to Boston may have freed him from immediate danger, but it did not rescue him from his destructive habits. He quickly became involved in Roxbury's gambling and numbers operations and also organized a burglary ring with Shorty. His former girlfriend Sophia and her sister scouted out potential targets for his thefts by acting as door-to-door saleswomen.

For a while, Malcolm made a good living by selling stolen goods to pawn shops. His theft ring was finally uncovered when he took a stolen watch to be repaired. The police, on the lookout for the watch, arrested him when he retrieved it at the shop, and he received a 10-year prison sentence for burglary. His hustler's luck had finally run out.

Malcolm had survived several brushes with death, and his wild life had given him a bitter knowledge of the worst of human behavior. Yet when he entered Boston's Charlestown State Prison in February 1946, he was only 20 years old.

4

Awakening

Malcolm endured a harrowing first few months at Charlestown State Prison. In prison slang, he was a fish (a new inmate), and he did not take well to being in the tank. He was placed in a tiny cell that had a covered bucket for a toilet. He was forced to follow the prison's dreary, inflexible daily routine while suffering withdrawal from the drugs he had been taking. His prisoner number was constantly drilled into him because the authorities never referred to a prisoner by his name.

The metal bars that surrounded Malcolm made him feel like a caged animal. He soon became sullen and defiant, throwing loud temper tantrums and cursing at both the prison psychologist and the chaplain. Eventually, when the guards called out his prison number at roll call in the morning, he refused to answer.

Malcolm was often placed in solitary confinement as the prison authorities tried to squash his rebelliousness. Yet the

Even after returning to Boston, Malcolm X continued his destructive habits. He was eventually arrested for burglary and received a sentence to serve ten years at Charlestown State Prison in Massachusetts, seen here in an earlier photo.

punishment did little to deter his violent behavior, partly because he liked the isolation. He would pace his cell furiously, lashing out at everyone and everything until he wore himself out. After resting for a while, he would get up and resume his attacks.

Malcolm took such perverse pride in his violent behavior and his status as an outcast that his fellow inmates gave him the nickname of Satan. He refused to conform to any aspect of prison life. The only thing that seemed to temporarily calm him were the mildly intoxicating spices that prisoners abused as substitutes for hard drugs.

Malcolm felt little beyond an intense hatred of himself and the world. His relatives tried to help him adjust. Ella sometimes met him in the prison's visiting room and his brothers and sisters wrote to him, but during his first two years in jail, he stubbornly resisted all their efforts to reach out to him.

It was a meeting with an older prisoner named Bimbi that would help Malcolm take a first step toward changing his life. A professional burglar and veteran of many prisons, Bimbi had used his time in jail to broaden his mind with the study of such subjects as grammar, history, and philosophy. He was held in great esteem by Charlestown's prisoners, especially because of the eloquence with which he defended his opinions.

Malcolm and Bimbi worked together in the prison workshop where license plates were stamped out. One day, when the prisoners had a short break from work, Malcolm made a blistering attack on religion. Bimbi demolished Malcolm's argument without raising his voice or cursing—Malcolm's usual tactics when debating an issue. Bimbi's words did not change Malcolm's views about religion, but it did show him how an intelligent and masterful speaker could take command of an audience.

The young inmate also discovered that he had impressed Bimbi as well. According to the older man, Malcolm had a fine mind, which he could improve by studying in the prison library and taking correspondence courses. Coming from a man whom Malcolm greatly respected, the advice struck home. He decided to enroll in a correspondence course in English grammar.

A WAY OUT OF PRISON

Because Malcolm had dropped out of school in the eighth grade, he had much catching up to do. His natural intelligence and curiosity helped him overcome many shortcomings, and he soon expanded his studies to include Latin and linguistics. Although his vocabulary and handwriting remained fairly crude, his ability to express his ideas improved bit by bit.

While Malcolm furthered his education, he also began to think about the twists and turns that had led him to a cell in Charlestown. He soon came to realize that broad political and social observations could be drawn from his experiences as a black youth struggling to find a place in American society. Slowly, he transformed himself from a self-centered hustler into a socially conscious black militant.

In 1948, a few months after Malcolm was transferred to a prison in Concord, Massachusetts, Ella persuaded state prison officials to move him to a more modern facility in nearby Norfolk, Massachusetts. The new prison operated under more relaxed rules and had a large library, flush toilets, and regular rooms instead of barred cells for each inmate. Malcolm took advantage of the prison's educational program, which featured lectures and debates led by instructors from local colleges, and steadily improved his speaking skills.

During his stay at the Norfolk Prison, Malcolm also developed an interest in religion. His brothers Reginald and Philbert and his sister Hilda had been writing to him for some time about the black religious group known as the Nation of Islam, which they had joined. Malcolm had always responded with crude, sarcastic insults when they told him that they had mentioned his name in prayer meetings. Slowly, though, he became intrigued. He knew he needed something other than rage to give meaning to his life, and he was interested in Reginald's promise that becoming a Black Muslim would ultimately be his ticket to freedom.

In late 1948, Reginald decided to try to lure Malcolm into the fold. He ended a letter to Malcolm with a mysterious proposition. "Don't eat any more pork, and don't smoke any more cigarettes," Reginald told his older brother. "I'll show you how to get out of prison."

Reginald's strange advice had an effect on Malcolm, although not the one Reginald intended. By neither eating pork nor smoking cigarettes (which are observances of the Islamic faith), he might be able to fool the authorities into thinking he had reformed. Perhaps they would then parole him from prison. After all, he had deceived an army psychiatrist once. Why not a prison psychiatrist?

Malcolm abstained from pork and cigarettes while he waited for a visit from Reginald, who was then to reveal the entire scheme. In prison, where the smallest changes in routine are the subject of endless gossip, Malcolm's action set off a chorus of whispers. "Satan doesn't eat pork!" the inmates told one another.

When Reginald finally paid a visit at Norfolk, Malcolm discovered that his brother did not have a magic dietary formula to help him get out of prison. All he had to offer was the Nation of Islam. In response to Malcolm's question about how abstinence from pork and cigarettes could free someone, Reginald offered another question: "If a man knew every imaginable thing that there is to know, who would he be?"

"Well, he would have to be some kind of a god," Malcolm answered.

Reginald replied that there was a man who knew everything. His name was Allah.

Puzzled, Malcolm listened as Reginald described how Allah had a full circle—360 degrees—of knowledge, whereas Allah's enemy, the devil, had only 33 degrees.

Most of Reginald's explanation of the Nation of Islam's teachings was baffling to Malcolm, but two phrases stuck in his mind: "The white man is the devil," and "The black man is brainwashed."

After Reginald left, Malcolm began to think deeply about his own experiences with whites. He and his family had been terrorized by the Ku Klux Klan and split up by white social workers; he had been exploited by white employers, harassed by white policemen, and jailed by white judges. Everywhere he had gone in the ghettos, he had seen poor blacks abandoned by white society.

Again, Malcolm spun through his head the two statements that were the opposite sides of the same coin in the Nation of Islam's theology: The white race was corrupt and was the source of all evil; the members of the black race were Allah's chosen people and were destined to destroy the white devils. To Malcolm, the statements seemed to offer a sound explanation for all the injustice in the world. Moreover, he took great comfort in the prediction that a terrifying doom awaited all whites. He found himself wanting to learn more about the Nation of Islam.

During the next few weeks, Reginald, Hilda, and Philbert wrote to Malcolm almost daily, discussing the philosophy of the Black Muslims and urging him to place himself in the hands of Allah and his supreme prophet, Elijah Muhammad, who headed the Nation of Islam. The more Malcolm learned about Islam, the more focused he felt. Hearing about the

IN HIS OWN WORDS...

Malcolm X's past provided him with a perspective that enabled him to reach out to those living in the ghettos, battling addictions, and struggling to find work. In his famous "The Ballot or the Bullet" speech, delivered on April 3, 1964, in Cleveland, Ohio, he said:

> No, I'm not an American. I'm one of the 22 million black people who are the victims of Americanism. One of the 22 million black people who are the victims of democracy, nothing but disguised hypocrisy. So I'm not standing here speaking to you as an American, or a patriot, or a flag-saluter, or a flag-waver—no, not I. I'm speaking as a victim of this American system. And I see America through the eyes of the victim. I don't see any American dream; I see an American nightmare.

supremacy of the black race sparked a sense of inner pride that he had rarely felt since the time when he had attended meetings of the Universal Negro Improvement Association with his father.

For years, Malcolm had been drifting through life without any direction. Now, if he wanted to join the Nation of Islam, he would have to accept its theology and submit completely to the authority of Elijah Muhammad. As Malcolm learned more about Elijah Muhammad and the teachings of the Nation of Islam, he saw many parallels with his father's life, and these associations made it easier for him to consider converting to Islam.

THE LIFE OF A PROPHET

Originally named Elijah Poole, Elijah Muhammad was born in 1897 in a rural Georgia community, about 70 miles from where Earl Little was born, and grew up with a strong belief in racial pride and black solidarity. Like Malcolm's father, he, too, moved north in search of better work opportunities and freedom from racial oppression. With his large family, he settled in Detroit.

In 1931, Poole met a small, brown-skinned man named W. D. Fard, who sold silk products door-to-door in Detroit's black ghetto. Fard claimed to be from Arabia and styled himself as a prophet who had come to the United States to help blacks discover their dual African and Islamic heritage. According to Fard, black Americans were descended from the first humans, the "original race," whose descendants could be found in their purest form among Muslims in the Middle East, Africa, and Asia. Fard told black Americans they were Islam's "lost sheep," and he said he and his Nation of Islam faith could help them find their true religion and overcome their white oppressors.

Fard's teachings varied markedly from those of traditional Islam, which teaches brotherhood between people of all races.

His religion had many beliefs in common with Marcus Garvey's black nationalist movement and Noble Drew Ali's early twentieth-century Islamic group, the short-lived Moorish Temple of America. Ali, who amassed a wide following by claiming that blacks were superior to whites and the white race was doomed, mysteriously disappeared sometime in the late 1920s. Fard's movement attracted some of the same people who had been drawn to Garvey and Ali.

One of Fard's first converts was Elijah Poole, who changed his name to Elijah Muhammad in accordance with Fard's command that his followers give up their Christian surnames and take Islamic names. Fard told blacks that their Christian surnames were false names because they were probably the names of slave owners who had robbed blacks of their true African names. Some converts used an *X* or combination of *X*s and other letters to symbolize that their true names had been lost and they had become *ex*-slaves.

Fard and Muhammad roused growing support for the Nation of Islam during the early 1930s and established Islamic temples (known as mosques) in converted stores in a number of Midwestern cities. The group's message of black superiority and resistance to white domination appealed especially to the poor blacks of the urban ghettos. Fard's religious doctrines offered these people hope that their hardships would soon end.

The scriptures that Fard preached were based on Islamic teachings, but they included a strong emphasis on racial doctrines. He taught there was no heaven or hell after death; instead, heaven and hell existed here on earth. Black Americans, according to Fard, had been living in hell for nearly 400 years. This period of slavery and damnation was coming to an end, however, because of the return of the savior for black Americans. In Islamic tradition, this savior is called the Madhi and is considered to be both a person and God. The Madhi, Fard taught, was none other than himself.

Elijah Muhammad became the leader of the Nation of Islam in 1934. His followers viewed him as the supreme prophet of the militant religion that preached that whites were corrupt and blacks were God's chosen people.

The Nation of Islam's beliefs about the beginnings of mankind differed sharply from those of any other religious group. According to Fard, the world was ruled in early times by members of a black race who were known as the original men. These people established a highly advanced civilization, and their scientists populated the earth with animals, created mountains and seas, blasted the moon into the sky from the Pacific Ocean region, and even communicated with a race of nine-foot-tall giants on Mars. The original men lived in peace with each other and worshiped Allah from their holy city of Mecca.

Fard taught that evil had entered the world because a mad scientist named Yacub had let his pride in his scientific knowledge tempt him into breaking the laws of Islam. Exiled from Mecca, the vengeful Yacub had used his knowledge of genetics to create a devil race of vicious, immoral white people. Once loosed upon the world, the lying and scheming white devils caused great trouble for the original people.

Eventually, the whites were herded together and sent to live in caves in the cold wasteland of Europe. Allah sent the black prophets Moses and Jesus to teach the white devils about Islam with the hope of civilizing them. According to Fard, the whites corrupted the prophets' teachings and created the religions of Judaism and Christianity.

Fard maintained that in accordance with an ancient prophecy, the white devils had finally gained control of the world. Once in power, no evil was beyond them. They had enslaved millions of blacks in Africa and transported them to the Americas, where the black captives were stripped of their language, culture, and history and were brainwashed into hating themselves. They were taught that whites were superior in all ways and that God and Jesus were white.

The corrupt reign of the white man was about to end, Fard said. He, the Madhi, had appeared, and he was going to lead the black race back to the original state of grace it had known before the advent of the white man. The time of redemption was at hand.

Fard's religious doctrines and claims to divine authority were called absurd by whites as well as by his black critics, yet they had a great emotional ring of truth to the people who swelled the membership of the Nation of Islam. His followers found his account of the history of mankind to be at least as believable as the one found in the Bible, which was often used by white racists to support their arguments that blacks were inferior. The Nation of Islam, with its message of racial pride and devotion to Allah, hoped to persuade blacks to build a separate society free from the control of whites.

The Nation of Islam's initial period of growth was checked in 1934, when Fard disappeared without a trace. In the aftermath of this mysterious occurrence, Elijah Muhammad became engaged in a battle with other ministers for control of the Nation of Islam. Jailed for three years after being convicted of draft evasion, he eventually gained leadership of the Nation of Islam. As news of his uplifting sermons spread by word of mouth through the black ghettos of Midwestern cities, his stature grew. To his devoted followers, Muhammad was known as "the Messenger," the man who would lead the faithful to the Kingdom of Allah. To Malcolm Little in Norfolk Prison, he seemed to be the man who could free him from his troubled past.

By late 1949, Malcolm had resolved the inner struggles that had propelled him both toward and away from Islam. Describing the tremendous impact that his conversion to Islam had on him, he said, "Every instinct of the ghetto jungle streets, every hustling fox and criminal wolf instinct in me, which would have scoffed at and rejected anything else, was struck numb." He compared his own experience with that of the apostle Paul, who had a similarly blinding revelation when he had converted to Christianity.

When Malcolm told his brothers and sisters that he had accepted Allah, they urged him to write immediately to Elijah Muhammad. It took him more than 25 attempts to write a letter that expressed exactly how he felt about his newfound faith. When he at last finished a draft that satisfied him, he mailed it off. Muhammad answered him promptly, welcoming Malcolm to the knowledge of Islam and telling him to have courage. Following the Nation of Islam's custom, 24-year-old Malcolm dropped his surname and replaced it with the letter X.

Having once been a hustler, a drug-dealer, and a thief, Malcolm now set himself on a course to become an active minister of the Nation of Islam and a committed fighter for black freedom and dignity. His ministry and his battle would have to begin, however, while he was still in prison.

5

Fishing for Souls

Armed with a militant new spiritual faith, Malcolm X began to search for his place within the Nation of Islam. He was amazed at how quickly his old habits and ways of thinking faded away, but some changes occurred only after a hard struggle. One of his most difficult tasks was learning how to pray in the Islamic fashion, humbly touching his head to the ground while kneeling in the direction of Mecca. "Picking a lock to rob someone's house was the only way my knees had been bent before," he said. Once he became comfortable with praying, however, he felt that another vestige of his past life had been swept away.

With Malcolm X's new religious beliefs came an even greater personal commitment to improving his mind. By the beginning of 1950, the reading program he had begun before his conversion to Islam had been in progress for a year. Yet he was still dissatisfied with his handwriting and vocabulary.

After converting to Islam, Malcolm X made a commitment to improving his mind by reading voraciously and practicing his writing. He evolved from a violent, rebellious person into someone introspective and charismatic. Prison authorities noticed this change and granted him parole in 1952 after he had served six years.

Determined to correct this weakness, he sat down at the desk in his room and began laboriously copying the first page of a dictionary. It took him all day to finish the task. He copied another page from the dictionary on the following day—and on every day thereafter for the next four years. By following this regimen, he not only improved his handwriting and vocabulary but trained himself to exercise self-discipline.

Malcolm X's strict adherence to his writing program was in keeping with the practices of the Nation of Islam. Mental, spiritual, and moral discipline are the great underlying strengths of the religion. Besides maintaining a careful and restricted diet, Black Muslims are required to be neatly dressed, well spoken, and respectful of others, especially other Muslims. Sexual promiscuity is strictly forbidden. No practitioner is allowed to drink alcohol or smoke cigarettes.

Malcolm X firmly followed all the Nation of Islam's strictures while making use of his growing skill as a writer. He sent letters to former underworld friends, urging them to follow in his footsteps, and to government officials about the need to fight racial injustice. Writing these letters helped him sort out the benefits of Islam for black Americans and fired his desire to bring the word of Allah to others. He wrote daily to his family in Michigan as well as to Elijah Muhammad about the progress he was making in understanding the teachings of Islam, and the two men built up a steady correspondence.

Malcolm X also engaged in a wide-ranging reading program. Every evening, he pored through books from the Norfolk prison library. After the lights in his room were turned off at 10 P.M., he would read by the light from the hallway. He usually read until 3 A.M., jumping into bed whenever the guards came by on their routine checks, then returning to his book after they had passed. "The ability to read," he said, "awoke in me some long dormant craving to be mentally alive."

Malcolm X began a comprehensive study of history, archaeology, religion, philosophy, and science. His readings included everything from discussions of the theory of genetics to documents about the pre–Civil War antislavery movement. Always reading with an eye for political content, he searched for examples of how the native populations of countries in Asia, Africa, and the Americas were exploited by foreign white rulers and how these peoples had built revolutionary movements to fight for their independence.

Two works that had a strong impact on Malcolm X and opened his eyes to the vast sweep of black American history were W.E.B. Du Bois's book *Souls of Black Folk* and Carter G.

Woodson's *Journal of Negro History*. From these and other sources, he learned about the ancient civilizations of Africa and about the enslavement of Africans by the Europeans. He also read about people who resisted slavery, including Nat

W.E.B. Du Bois

While in prison, Malcolm X read *The Souls of Black Folk* by W.E.B. Du Bois. The forceful writing impressed Malcolm X, who agreed with Du Bois's strong stand in support of those who actively demanded equal rights.

William Edward Burghardt Du Bois was born in 1868 in Massachusetts. He was an avid student, and, unlike many other African Americans of his time, was able to achieve his dream of higher education. He graduated from Fisk University before becoming the first African American to earn a Ph.D. from Harvard. He then spent two years studying at the University of Berlin in Germany.

Du Bois returned to America impressed by the greater racial tolerance he had experienced while in Germany and determined to change the status of African Americans in his native country. He founded the Niagara Movement with other African-American leaders who shared his determination to bring about racial equality and later became active in the newly founded National Association for the Advancement of Colored People (NAACP), the only African American chosen to serve on the organization's first board of directors. For many years, Du Bois served as editor of the NAACP's magazine, the *Crisis*, and his passionate editorials and strong editorial positions in the magazine often forced a more activist stance for the organization.

Du Bois wrote extensively on the experiences and attitudes of African Americans. He fought bitterly with Booker T. Washington, who Du Bois believed was accommodating racist attitudes rather than trying to create change.

Du Bois was one of the foremost intellectuals of the civil rights movement. Unlike many of his contemporaries in the civil rights movement, he was highly educated, was not religious, and benefited from having many supportive white contacts and mentors.

Du Bois gradually grew disillusioned with the possibility of achieving change in the United States. He moved to Africa, revoking his American citizenship, and became a citizen of Ghana shortly before his death.

Turner and other American slave revolt leaders. They provided him with powerful examples of black militancy.

The more Malcolm X read, the more he was able to find personal insights that helped him understand the teachings of Elijah Muhammad. He had only to think back to the one-paragraph summary of black history printed in the textbooks used by his junior high school classes to be reminded of Muhammad's statement that America had "whitened" its own history. The textbooks barely mentioned the horrors of the African slave trade and ignored the considerable achievements of black Americans—subjects that were highlighted in the Nation of Islam's teachings.

As he filled in the gaps in his knowledge, Malcolm X became increasingly confident he had the intellectual gifts necessary to be an effective preacher for the Nation of Islam. He spent less time in his room, took a more active role in prison activities, and engaged in formal debates with other inmates. Gradually, he drew other black prisoners into discussions about the teachings of the Nation of Islam. His fellow inmates were amazed at his change from a God-hating fanatic to an equally zealous preacher for Islam. Nevertheless, some of them began to listen to him.

Malcolm X was well suited for his role as a prison preacher. He knew how to speak to black prisoners: He was one of them. A product of the black ghettos (as were most of the inmates), he knew what kinds of statements would catch their attention. By skillfully mixing talk about the past glories of African civilizations with attacks on America's white-dominated institutions, he was able to interest a number of prisoners in the teachings of the Nation. As he wrote later, "The 'white man is the devil' is the perfect echo of that black convict's lifelong experience."

Malcolm X suffered a great shock when Elijah Muhammad expelled his brother Reginald from the Nation because it was discovered that he was having an affair with a female member of the Nation. The prison preacher grew even more troubled when Reginald visited him in prison after the expulsion and made a number of charges against Muhammad and the manner in which he was operating the Nation. Malcolm X realized that his loyalties were being severely tested. One man had introduced him to Islam; the other man was his spiritual adviser.

Hoping to patch up the rift between Reginald and the Nation, Malcolm X wrote a letter to Muhammad in which he defended his brother and asked for forgiveness. The following night, he experienced a vision in his prison cell. As he lay in his bed, a man with light brown skin and Asiatic features appeared before him and seated himself on a chair. The man looked at the inmate for a while and then disappeared. Malcolm X believed that the man was W. D. Fard, and his presence meant the troubled prisoner should remain utterly faithful to the Nation.

Muhammad stated in his response to Malcolm X's letter that the correct decision had been made about Reginald, and he counseled his follower to accept the verdict and go on with his studies. "If you once believed the truth, and now you are beginning to doubt the truth," Muhammad wrote, "then you didn't believe the truth in the first place." Muhammad's stand on the matter was an inflexible one, but it left Malcolm X reassured. There was only one truth, and he would follow it. His brother would have to make his own separate peace with the Nation of Islam.

The improvement in Malcolm X's character after his conversion to Islam was duly noted by prison authorities. In August 1952, at the age of 27, he was released from the penitentiary. He had served 6 years of his 10-year sentence.

One of the conditions of Malcolm X's parole was that he have a job waiting for him. His brother Wilfred, who was the manager of a furniture business in Detroit, arranged for him to work at the store. "I never looked back," he said after walking past the prison gates.

FISHING FOR ALLAH

Malcolm X's first purchases outside of prison—a pair of eye-glasses, a suitcase, and a wristwatch—were necessities that also had great symbolic importance attached to them. He needed glasses because he had damaged his eyes by reading in poor light, yet he felt they were fitting for someone who had a new focus on life. Sensing that he might be traveling frequently in the years ahead, he believed his new suitcase would become his constant companion.

The decision to wear a watch was perhaps the most telling sign of the radical change in Malcolm X's personality. In his days as a hustler, he had sometimes worn an expensive, flashy watch for show. When he was released from prison, the watch became a symbol for him of time ticking away. The gravity of his mission to spread the word about the Nation weighed on him, and he knew that winning converts in the black ghettos would not be an easy task. Too many years of his life had been wasted, and he was obsessed with the need to work fast.

After having his hair cropped short in the Black Muslim style, Malcolm X left Boston immediately after his release from prison and traveled to his brother Wilfred's house in Detroit. "The warmth of a home and a family was a healing change from the prison cage for me," he said. "It would deeply move almost any newly freed convict, I think. But especially this Muslim home's atmosphere sent me often to my knees to praise Allah."

Malcolm X worked as a furniture salesman in the store that Wilfred managed, and the business practices of the store's white owners, who sold low-quality furniture to black ghetto dwellers on credit at exorbitant interest rates, gave the new employee further insights into the ways in which the poor were exploited. The store owners masked their involvement in the store by hiring black managers and salesmen, and they knew that their poorly educated customers would be unable to read the fine print about high interest rates in the sales agreements. The exploitative practices enraged Malcolm X, who wrote, "I watched brothers entwining themselves in the economic clutches of the white man who went home every night with another bag of money drained from the ghetto." He soon left the furniture store to work in an automobile factory.

Although Malcolm X found little satisfaction in his work, he was nearly ecstatic to be within the welcoming fellowship of the Nation of Islam community in Detroit. He plunged into the group's activities at rituals at Temple Number One, the first mosque to have been established by Fard and Elijah Muhammad. Malcolm X was deeply impressed by the dignity and love he found both in his brother's home and at the temple. The community members exuded a radiant spirit that was much different from the feelings he had found elsewhere. He wrote, "I had never dreamed of anything like that atmosphere among black people who had learned to be proud they were black." During this period, the Nation of Islam's recruiting efforts had been meeting with only moderate success. Malcolm X was surprised that the temple usually had many empty seats at its prayer meetings. Nearly bursting with pride in his newfound faith, he could not believe that more blacks did not jump to embrace the Nation's message. He realized that a much more effective recruiting campaign was needed to get the word of Allah to the people.

Shortly after he arrived in Michigan, Malcolm X had his first meeting with Elijah Muhammad, the man whom he revered for saving him from a life of crime and despair. Malcolm X visited the Messenger at his home in Chicago and was almost overcome with his feelings of awe for the gentle, fatherly man. When they began to discuss the Nation of Islam, Malcolm X could not help voicing his disappointment about the lack of active members in the Detroit temple. Muhammad, sensing the young convert's dynamism, agreed with his observation. "Go after the young people," Muhammad instructed. "Once you get them the older ones will follow."

As he read and learned about Islam, Malcolm X became confident that he had the gifts necessary to become an effective preacher for the Nation of Islam. He was passionate about helping other black Americans acquire the same faith he had found, and Elijah Muhammad saw him as a star pupil. Here, Muhammad introduced Malcolm X before a speech in Chicago in 1961.

Taking the Messenger's advice to heart, Malcolm X went "fishing," the term that Black Muslims used for their recruiting expeditions. He made circuits of Detroit's pool halls, bar-rooms, and street corners, engaging young men with a bit of opening ghetto slang to get their attention: "My man, let me pull your coat on something." Many people shied away from him as if he were a crazy man. Others listened spellbound as he talked about the power and beauty of the black race and of how Allah was soon going to sweep the white man from the face of the earth.

Malcolm X would speak until he was hoarse, and afterwards he would pace the streets for hours, brooding about ways to reach the souls of black Americans who would not listen to him. They were people whose hair was conked, who sought to deny their black heritage, and who were destroying themselves with drugs and alcohol. These men and women reminded him of his own past, and he vowed to help them find the same strong spiritual faith that he had found.

Within a few months, Malcolm X almost single-handedly tripled the membership of Temple Number One. By mixing his attacks on whites with humorous analogies that urged his listeners to stop imitating their white oppressors and stop depending on white charities, he won them over. "The man who tosses worms in the river isn't necessarily a friend of the fish," he told his audiences. "All the fish who took him for a friend, who think the worm's got no hooks in it, usually end up on the frying pan."

By luring recruits with sharp words and a barbed wit, Malcolm X apparently had the most effective hooks of all.

6

The Pure Flame of Allah

Malcolm X's success in filling the benches of the Nation of Islam's Detroit temple earned him an appointment as assistant minister there in 1953. Burning with religious and political fervor, he decided to quit his job at the automobile factory and devote all his time to missionary work. He traveled frequently to Chicago to speak with Elijah Muhammad and study at the library in the Messenger's home.

More and more, Muhammad looked on Malcolm X as his star pupil. He was a natural leader, with magnetic charm and an aura of spirituality that drew people to the temples. The Nation was having a hard time getting its message to a large audience and strongly needed a preacher who could appeal to the black masses in the cities. Malcolm X seemed to Muhammad like the perfect choice.

In 1953, Muhammad gave Malcolm X his first major assignment: Organize a temple in Boston. Before he could leave

Detroit, he was visited by FBI agents who questioned him about the Nation and about why he had not registered with his military draft board. With the Korean War in progress, all men over the age of 18 and a half were required to register for service in the armed forces.

Malcolm X went directly to the local draft board and declared himself a conscientious objector to service in the military. When asked if he knew the meaning of "conscientious objection," he replied, "When the white man [asks] me to go somewhere and fight and maybe die to preserve the way the white man [treats] the black man in America, then my conscience objects." He received a deferred status and heard nothing more from the army.

Malcolm X began his new ministry in Boston preaching in the living room of a fellow Black Muslim. While in the city, he visited many of his old friends in Roxbury. Quite a few of them were distrustful of his new Islamic beliefs. The "wire," as street gossip was called, was reporting that Malcolm X was on a "religious kick," and his old hustling friends suspected he was operating another of the storefront confidence games that were common throughout the ghetto. Malcolm X realized that his friends were not ready to accept what he was preaching, so he did not attempt to convert them.

Within three months of his arrival in Boston, Malcolm X had organized a thriving Nation of Islam community, which met in its own small temple. Pleased with his minister's success, Muhammad sent him to Philadelphia to establish another temple. Again, Malcolm X quickly gathered a group of converts to Islam. Before long, the Nation had its 12th temple, and Malcolm X was recognized as the group's rising star.

Because of his superb preaching, which he had constantly refined during his "fishing" expeditions, Malcolm X was often referred to as the Nation's "hard hitting young minister." He could preach for hours, and he often did. His message—the word of Elijah Muhammad—was always the same, and it was

By 1953, Malcolm X had quit his job in order to devote all his time to acting as a missionary for the Nation of Islam. He was an integral part in the growth of the organization and soon became well known throughout the country. Here, Malcolm X addresses a rally in Harlem in 1963.

usually peppered with references to the evil deeds of whites and the coming apocalypse that would utterly destroy them.

Malcolm X also preached about the need for blacks to unify and reach out to each other. He told his audiences to feel enraged about the indignities they had to endure at the hands of whites, to liberate themselves from their feelings of self-hatred and worthlessness, and to take pride in their black heritage. Speaking to his temple congregations, he said, "We all have in common the greatest binding tie we could have— we all are black people."

Malcolm accused all white Americans of racism. He held out little hope that their attitude toward blacks would change. The liberties that white Americans prized for themselves, even during the years when slavery was practiced in the United States, would never be fully extended to blacks. "We didn't land on the Plymouth Rock, my brothers and sisters," he said, "Plymouth Rock landed on us!" To get out from under that rock, he preached, blacks must throw off their dependence on whites and build a separate society. In addition, he said, blacks must worship according to the beliefs of their own special religion, the Nation of Islam.

In June 1954, as a reward for his hard work, Malcolm X was appointed to head Temple Number Seven in New York City. The temple was located in the most depressed area of Harlem, yet he was ecstatic about the assignment. He had come full circle. Only 10 years before, he had been one of the most deluded and desperate hustlers in the district. Now he returned as a minister, a pure flame of Allah, to ignite a revolution in the largest black community in America.

At first, Malcolm X had trouble getting the Nation's message heard because other groups in Harlem were also preaching that blacks should turn their backs on white society. With his customary energy, though, he traveled through the ghetto's streets and soon began to pull hundreds of new converts into the Nation. Among his best sources for recruits were the small, storefront Christian churches that lined the streets of Harlem's poorest areas. He and his assistants waited until the church services were over and then pounced on the congregants with the message that Christianity was a slave master's religion. After listening to him preach, many former Baptists and Catholics became devout Muslims.

Temple Number Seven grew quickly, but not swiftly enough for Malcolm X. Besides preaching six or seven nights a week at temple meetings and on Harlem street corners, he organized a nightly adult education course, during which he led debates about current events and religious topics. He also found the time to preach regularly in Philadelphia and logged many miles on the road as he drove to Springfield, Massachusetts; Hartford, Connecticut; and Atlanta, Georgia, to organize new temples.

By 1957, Malcolm X was traveling to the West Coast and starting temples in Los Angeles and other western cities. He ultimately had a hand in the formation of more than two dozen new congregations throughout the country. By the end of the 1950s, the Nation became a formidable presence in the ghettos of the nation's biggest cities thanks largely to his inexhaustible energy.

FRUIT OF ISLAM

The Nation was a relatively poor organization whose members often lived from hand to mouth during the mid-1950s. Gradually, however, the Nation's financial situation changed as its membership grew, for all members were required to make substantial monetary contributions to the organization. The group began to buy real estate and start small businesses. Some members ran farms, while others operated bakeries, clothing stores, and even small factories. The profits from these business ventures helped the Nation expand its ministry and build a large temple headquarters in Chicago.

The membership of the Nation, which in the group's early years had been drawn mainly from the poorest blacks and reformed convicts such as Malcolm X, began to include converts from the educated middle class. The adult males of each of the Nation's temples composed a tightly organized corps known as the Fruit of Islam, and they attended weekly sessions to receive instruction in religious doctrine, moral issues, and self-defense techniques. The female members of the Nation, known as the Muslim Sisters, were held in great respect, but were expected to play a subordinate role to the men.

The Nation's strict moral code and the iron discipline it exerted over its members frightened away some potential converts. Yet when Malcolm X was recruiting, he used these aspects of the organization to his advantage. He told ghetto residents that whites preferred blacks to remain disorganized, lazy, and demoralized because then they were easier to control. He often directed his message at the silent black masses in urban slums, hoping to harness their rage for a holy war against the "blue-eyed devils."

Malcolm X did not use just angry words to stir up his audiences. He also encouraged them to focus a rational eye on their situations and find clearheaded solutions to their problems. He referred to this process of breaking down complex issues as "cracking atoms," and he often used this line of deductive reasoning to demonstrate the methods by which blacks were forced to remain second-class citizens.

As the recruiting efforts of Malcolm X and other Black Muslim ministers became increasingly successful, the organization began to hold national meetings. Members from around the country gathered in Chicago every year on Savior's Day, February 26, to celebrate the birthday of W. D. Fard. The Nation also staged huge rallies, known as Living Fountain assemblies, in many cities. Malcolm X was the organizing force behind these gatherings, and his dynamic speaking presence often overshadowed the official focus of the assemblies: Elijah Muhammad, the Living Fountain.

The Nation's growth in the 1950s occurred at a time when enormous changes seemed to be in store for race relations in the United States. While Malcolm X was delivering his black separatist message to audiences in the ghettos, a young minister named Martin Luther King, Jr., was leading a boycott of segregated bus services in Montgomery, Alabama. Throughout the South, civil rights organizations, such as the Southern Christian Leadership Conference (SCLC) and the Congress on Racial Equality (CORE), were challenging racial segregation in public schools and theaters, in restaurants and rest rooms, on trains and buses. Although the nonviolent protest marches led by King and his colleagues often met with brutal retaliation from white policemen and white supremacist organizations, the civil rights movement was beginning to have some success in eroding racial discrimination in the South. (For additional information on these civil rights organizations, enter "Southern Christian Leadership Conference" or "Congress on Racial Equality" into any search engine and browse the sites listed.)

The civil rights marchers won much praise for their courageous fight for racial integration, but not from Malcolm X. He had nothing but contempt for their goals and tactics. "You can sit down next to white folks—on the toilet," he remarked, belittling recent rulings outlawing segregated rest rooms. He told those who championed integration, "The masses of black people want a society of their own in a land of their own." Criticizing nonviolent protest methods that required blacks to sacrifice their bodies and sometimes their lives in fighting for their constitutional rights, he called for blacks to defend themselves when attacked—bullet for bullet, if necessary.

By 1957, Malcolm X's militant ideas had begun to attract some fervent advocates in the Northern black ghettos. The Nation's membership numbered around 1,000 at this time, and he was able to call on a cadre of 60 or 70 hard-core Muslim activists for rallies that he held in the streets of Harlem. The New York Police Department, which kept tabs on groups deemed to be potentially troublesome, had files on some of the Black Muslims. Many of the city's leaders, though—even some of its black ones—had never heard of the group. That all changed one April evening in 1957.

That night, on a Harlem street, the police broke up a fight. While making their arrests, the police brusquely ordered the bystanders to move on. Several members of Temple Number Seven were among those watching the incident, and they refused to move. They wanted to make sure that the men who

During the same period as the growth of the Nation of Islam, civil rights organizations were challenging segregation in the South. In this photograph, members of the "Freedom Riders," a group sponsored by the Congress of Racial Equality that tried to desegregate public buses, sit outside a Greyhound bus set on fire by a white mob. Malcolm X was opposed to the peaceful tactics of this and other civil rights groups and called for blacks to defend themselves if attacked.

had just been arrested would not be beaten by the police. Angered by the Muslims' obstinacy, the police attacked one of them, a man named Hinton Johnson, and opened up a large gash in his scalp. He was then arrested and taken to police precinct headquarters, where he was thrown into a cell.

Less than an hour later, 50 members of the Fruit of Islam, with Malcolm X at the head of the group, stood in military formation outside the precinct house where Johnson was being held. They remained absolutely silent and created an eerie scene that was part confrontation and part vigil. Their defiant stance quickly attracted a large crowd of onlookers.

Harlem had been the site of many riots and murders before, but its residents had never witnessed a show of defiance and solidarity quite like this one. Blacks were not in the habit of directly confronting the police. In fact, the police were also drawn to the display and came to the windows of the precinct building to stare at the Black Muslims.

Finally, Malcolm X went into the precinct house and demanded to see Johnson. At first, the police refused to let him see the beaten man, but they were getting nervous because of the growing crowd outside, and they finally gave in to Malcolm's request.

As soon as Malcolm X saw the condition Johnson was in, he demanded that the badly injured man be taken to Harlem Hospital. An angry crowd followed the ambulance to the hospital and waited outside until they heard that Johnson was receiving proper medical care. Upon being told that the injured man was being treated, Malcolm X made a gesture to the crowd, and the people instantly dispersed. One white policeman who was at the scene was heard to say, "This is too much power for one man to have."

The Johnson incident made headlines not only in New York's leading black newspaper, the *Amsterdam News*, but also in the city's major dailies. With their show of strength outside the station house, the Black Muslims were letting the Harlem community know that the relationship between its police force and its inhabitants was changing. Harlemites started to look upon Malcolm X and the Nation of Islam with awe, a feeling that increased when Johnson and the Nation sued the police and won a large settlement. By then, the Black Muslims were a force to be reckoned with in Harlem. Politicians and community leaders thought it best not to make any critical statements that would spark a mass impromptu street rally of the group and its supporters.

Malcolm's voice was rapidly becoming the most feared—and perhaps the best loved—in Harlem. Yet he knew there was a much larger theater waiting. The nationwide struggle against racial oppression was just heating up, and he was burning to be a part of it. Calling out to black Americans to throw off the shackles of passivity and self-deprecation, he preached, "My black brothers and sisters—no one will know who we are . . . until we know who we are."

Malcolm X wanted to be known as more than an outspoken preacher. If he became a spokesman of the frustration and anger of ghetto blacks, though, he would be taking on a difficult—and dangerous—role.

7

Thunder in the Ghetto

At the age of 34, Malcolm X emerged as an extremely important figure in the Nation of Islam's affairs. Elijah Muhammad was suffering from bronchial asthma, so Malcolm X toured Africa in 1959 as the organization's ambassador and established relations with Muslim groups in Egypt and other countries on the African continent. Newspaper and television reporters anxious to hear the Nation's opinion on developments in racial relations in the United States began seeking him out, and he was ready and willing to serve as the group's sharp-tongued spokesman.

The Nation had emerged from relative obscurity at a time when racial discrimination was one of the most hotly debated issues in America. Malcolm X, Elijah Muhammad, and the Nation became especially visible after being featured on "The Hate That Hate Produced," a television documentary that aired in 1959. Narrated by journalist Mike Wallace, the program showed how violently the Black Muslims and their supporters resented white society and was filled with graphic evidence that a firestorm was gathering in the country's black ghettos. It was a shocking revelation to most white Americans, who had no inkling that discontent among blacks ran so deep.

Looking to further publicize the Nation's views, Malcolm X started publishing a newspaper, *Muhammad Speaks*, in the basement of his home. This weekly periodical, which printed the sayings of Elijah Muhammad along with relentless attacks on white racism, was an immediate success in the black community and eventually became the largest-circulating black publication in the country, with a circulation of more than a half million. The papers were sold by the members of the Fruit of Islam.

At the helm of Temple Number Seven, Malcolm X remained a study in contrasts. Always neatly dressed in a dark suit and narrow tie, he hardly looked the part of a ghetto warrior. His speech combined the latest street slang with his now-vast vocabulary. He thrived on highly emotional appeals to his audience, yet he was also known for having a cool head, logical thoughts, and an unshakable nerve. Some people found him aloof, cynical, and combative; others were impressed by his deep love for the black race and the compassion he showed for the poor and homeless.

Malcolm X's character had taken a turn in 1958, when he married Betty X (later known as Betty Shabazz), a nurse and teacher at the Nation's New York temple. The marriage startled his friends because he had never hesitated to express his deep distrust of women—though he always said women should be treated with respect. Yet he clearly trusted Betty, an understanding, supportive wife who knew that the black struggle came first in her husband's life.

Malcolm and Betty's first child, Attilah, was born in 1958. They eventually had five more daughters: Quibilah, Ilyasah, Gamilah, Malaak, and Malikah. A loving husband and father, he regretted that his hectic schedule often took him away from his family for weeks at a time. He treasured the moments they

Malcolm X published a newspaper, *Muhammad Speaks*, from the basement of his home, in hopes of further spreading the beliefs of the Nation of Islam. This Black Muslim holds an issue of the paper from 1964, which printed the sayings of Elijah Muhammad and attacked white racism.

spent together at their home in East Elmhurst, located in the New York City borough of Queens.

The living conditions in Harlem were such that Malcolm X was unwilling to raise a family there, yet the ghetto remained the focus of his life. The anger he felt as he looked at the broken homes and heard the despairing voices gave him the strength of spirit he needed to campaign on behalf of the powerless and forgotten people of the black ghettos. Other black American leaders may have been heartened by the sight of the civil rights marches in the South, but Malcolm X refused to feel optimistic about the nation's slow progress in improving racial relations. "The black masses are living a nightmare," he insisted.

Malcolm X's greatest hope was to foster a black revolution. Crowds of his supporters held rallies on Harlem's Lenox Avenue (later renamed Malcolm X Avenue) and heard him demand that America live up to its promise of freedom and justice for its black citizens. "White people," he said, "need someone to tell them what time it is." His view was that there was only one solution to the country's racial problems: Black Americans must unite and form a separate nation, either within the United States or in Africa. Until blacks lived free from white domination, he said, America would not have any peace.

IN HIS OWN WORDS...

Malcolm X's fiery speeches denouncing an American society dominated by whites made him a popular, if controversial, public speaker. On November 19, 1963, in Detroit, Michigan, he delivered his "Message to the Grass Roots" speech, in which he reminded his audience:

> You are nothing but a [sic] ex-slave. You don't like to be told that. But what else are you? You are ex-slaves. You didn't come here on the "Mayflower." You came here on a slave ship—in chains, like a horse, or a cow, or a chicken. And you were brought here by the people who came here on the "Mayflower." You were brought here by the so-called Pilgrims, or Founding Fathers. They were the ones who brought you here.
>
> We have a common enemy. We have this in common: We have a common oppressor, a common exploiter, and a common discriminator. But once we all realize that we have this common enemy, then we unite on the basis of what we have in common. And what we have foremost in common is that enemy—the white man. He's an enemy to all of us. I know some of you all think that some of them aren't enemies. Time will tell.

The 1960s began with Malcolm X continuing to dream of a revolution that would produce a separate nation for blacks. At the same time, a new force was taking hold of the civil rights movement: activist groups such as the Student Nonviolent Coordinating Committee (SNCC), formed by many of the young people who had marched with Martin Luther King, Jr., in Montgomery. Although they still believed in King's non-violent tactics, the students turned to more confrontational methods to protest against segregation and racial violence in the South. Their aggressive protest actions helped to boost black pride throughout the country, and Malcolm X welcomed their aggressive spirit.

As the 1960s progressed, sweeping changes in the nation's racial attitudes failed to materialize, and the high hopes of the civil rights marchers from the 1950s began to wane. More and more blacks, especially young blacks in the Northern ghettos, started to share Malcolm X's view that the campaign of non-violent resistance was yielding minimal results. His supporters could be heard humming "White Man's Heaven Is a Black Man's Hell," a popular song recorded by Louis X (today known as Louis Farrakhan), a former calypso singer who had become the minister of the Nation's Boston temple.

Thousands of militant young blacks flocked to hear Malcolm X's radical message. Journalists hounded him for his opinions about America's race relations, and he obliged them with his usual controversial statements. Styling himself as the uncom-promising champion of the black masses, he was relentless in attacking any social program that stopped short of demanding black liberation. When white leaders told him to be patient, he answered that blacks had waited long enough for com-pensation, and added an ominous warning: We do not forget, we do not forgive.

Malcolm X thrived on battling verbally with his critics. They accused him of being a violent revolutionary, an extremist, a demagogue who used emotionalism to obscure the issues, a hatemonger who was stirring up bad blood between whites and blacks. He responded that he was engaged in a war to free blacks from the misguided policies of more moderate black

Louis Farrakhan

In the 1960s, Malcolm X's fiery speeches were echoed by the lyrics of a young calypso singer who had joined the Nation of Islam. He recorded a song, "A White Man's Heaven is a Black Man's Hell"; changed his name first to Louis X and then to Louis Farrakhan; and became one of the most controversial leaders of the Nation of Islam.

Farrakhan was born in New York on May 11, 1933. He attended Winston-Salem Teachers College before working as a calypso singer. In 1955, he joined the Nation of Islam, ultimately moving to New York to work with Elijah Muhammad and Malcolm X. When Malcolm X left the Nation of Islam in 1964, Farrakhan replaced him as minister of Mosque Number Seven in Harlem.

A split in the membership of the Nation of Islam occurred with the death of Elijah Muhammad in 1975. Farrakhan served as head of the Nation of Islam, and Muhammad's son formed a new group, known as the Muslim American Community.

Farrakhan has become a controversial, if highly visible, leader of the Nation of Islam. Many of his speeches have been marked by rhetoric considered racist, sexist, and anti-Semitic. In 1983, Farrakhan supported Jesse Jackson during his campaign for the presidency, often appearing with Jackson at campaign rallies and speeches, until his anti-Semitic comments began to cause problems for the Jackson campaign. Farrakhan ultimately was asked to leave the Jackson campaign, and Jackson was forced to publicly distance himself from the controversial leader.

In 1995, Qubilah Shabazz, the daughter of Malcolm X, was accused of plotting to murder Farrakhan following her mother's public accusation that Farrakhan was involved in Malcolm X's assassination. In that same year, Farrakhan organized the Million Man March, a highly successful gathering of hundreds of thousands of African-American men in Washington. The march's stated aim—to unify a million "committed, dedicated, inspired black men for a day of atonement"—was extremely popular, but Farrakhan's speeches alienated as many as the march attracted. He remains a highly controversial leader of the Nation of Islam.

leaders, whom he scathingly described as "men with black bodies and white heads." He ridiculed anyone who believed the American government would agree to major racial reforms without the threat of a massive black uprising. Revolutions, he noted pointedly, are rarely bloodless.

Even though he called for blacks to denounce whites, Malcolm X was uncomfortable being depicted as a man who preached hate. He saw himself as some one who was seeking to promote unity among Muslims and blacks, not as a violent fanatic. Yet when he was questioned about his views, he often gave blunt answers that offended many people, both black and white. He believed there is no such thing as "bad" publicity and used the media to spread his reputation.

Malcolm X's confrontational manner made him a tremendous success as a public speaker. Audiences enjoyed his abrasive style so much that he became one of the most popular speakers on the college lecture circuit. There he discovered that many white students applauded his efforts and seemed to be genuinely committed to solving the country's racial problems. He held out the hope that the younger generation would not repeat the mistakes of their elders.

A RIFT FORMS

In 1962, with Elijah Muhammad still plagued by poor health, Malcolm X was appointed the national minister of the Nation of Islam. In this role, he was officially recognized as acting prime minister for Muhammad and heir apparent to the group's leadership. His appointment, however, aroused the jealousy of other Black Muslims—among them John Ali—who wanted to head the Nation, and Malcolm X soon began to suspect his rivals were turning Muhammad against him.

Initially, all Malcolm X heard were rumors that he was trying to usurp power from Muhammad. Then his name and picture began to appear less frequently in *Muhammad Speaks*, the editing and production of which had been taken away from him and reassigned to the Nation's headquarters in Chicago. Next, he was told by Muhammad to decline all invitations to appear on prominent television news broadcasts. Clearly, a rift was forming between the Messenger and his onetime favorite minister.

Events in the larger political arena were also troubling Malcolm X at this time. In April 1962, a confrontation between Black Muslims and police in Los Angeles left one group member dead and a dozen others wounded. Malcolm X wanted to retaliate by attacking the police, but the Nation's other leaders were unwilling to risk further trouble and forbade him to do anything more than make angry speeches. He perceived this as a weak response and believed many people would begin to question whether the Black Muslims deserved their militant reputation.

As the infighting continued, Malcolm X remained the heart and soul of militant black resistance for many ghetto dwellers even though he was on bad terms with the majority of the mainstream black leaders. In August 1963, when more than 200,000 people gathered in Washington, D.C., to sing hymns and march in support of racial understanding and greater civil rights legislation, he watched the demonstration from the sidelines and called the march a wasted effort. He told reporters, "I don't believe we're going to overcome [by] singing. If you're going to get yourself a .45 and start singing 'We Shall Overcome,' I'm with you."

Although Malcolm X was pessimistic about the value of peaceful protest marches, pressure from civil rights groups eventually persuaded Congress to pass a number of major bills outlawing a wide range of racially discriminatory practices. Among them were the Civil Rights Act of 1964 and the Economic Opportunity Act. Yet he continued to insist that the new laws were only showpieces and would not lead to any substantial improvements for blacks. "You don't stick a knife in a man's back nine inches and pull it out six inches and say you're making progress," he argued. Black America was still seething, according to him, and he pointed to recent outbreaks of racial violence in Northern cities as signs that the ghettos were about to erupt.

By the end of 1963, however, Malcolm X had to set aside all thoughts of a revolution as he engaged in a tremendous political battle within the Nation of Islam. He had heard rumors earlier in the year that Elijah Muhammad had fathered four children by two women who were his former secretaries. The women were serving Muhammad with a paternity suit, and Malcolm X found his faith in the Nation greatly shaken because adultery was a grave violation of Muslim ethics. He spoke to Muhammad's two accusers, and they not only provided him with evidence to back up their claims but also told him that Muhammad had predicted that his dynamic chief assistant would someday turn against him.

When Malcolm X confronted Muhammad on the matter, the Messenger did not deny the accusations but justified his actions by comparing himself with such biblical figures as David and Noah, who also had moral lapses. Muhammad's excuse did not satisfy Malcolm X, but there was little he could do about it. The only result of the incident was an increase in his alienation from Muhammad.

Malcolm X's troubles soon grew. On November 22, 1963, President John F. Kennedy was assassinated in Dallas, Texas, and the entire nation deeply mourned the loss of its popular leader. Yet in discussing the tragedy, Malcolm X stated that "the chickens [have] come home to roost," meaning that whites were being repaid for establishing a climate of violence in America. The comment created an uproar throughout the United States.

Muhammad realized that a convenient time had come to deal with Malcolm X's threat to his leadership. He suspended the national minister from his duties for a period of 90 days. While Malcolm X was faithfully obeying the suspension, he encountered more troubling news: Some Black Muslims were plotting to murder him for his alleged rebellion against the

Mainstream black leaders and civil rights activists achieved many successes in the early 1960s through protests and marches, like the NAACP march seen here, led by Martin Luther King, Jr. Malcolm X, however, remained skeptical about peaceful protesting tactics and the effect of new anti-discrimination legislature.

Messenger. He had often received death threats from white hate groups, but it stunned him to hear that his Muslim brothers would conspire to kill him. Shaken by these events, he wrote, "I felt like something in nature had failed—like the sun or the stars."

In January 1964, Muhammad summoned Malcolm X to Chicago to face charges that he was planning a rebellion. Among his accusers at the hearing were his chief rivals within the Nation. Knowing that a decision on the case would not be rendered for several months, Muhammad sent him to New York with the orders, "Go back and put out the fire you started." Otherwise, he was to keep his distance from other members of the Nation.

Malcolm X knew that chances for a reconciliation with Muhammad were fading fast. In February 1964, he and his family went to Miami, Florida, to stay with Cassius Clay, a widely popular boxer who had not yet announced to the public that he had converted to Islam and had changed his name to Muhammad Ali. Malcolm X would help the 22-year-old fighter prepare for his heavyweight title bout against the reigning champion, Sonny Liston. He hoped Muhammad would approve of the association, which brought a lot of publicity to the Nation, and reinstate him. Clay won the fight in six rounds, then announced his conversion and name change on the following day. Yet the Messenger remained at odds with Malcolm X.

A member of Temple Number Seven told Malcolm X upon his return to New York that the Nation's headquarters had sent word he should be killed. The fiery minister believed only one man

DID YOU KNOW?

Malcolm X's forceful personality and compelling speaking manner inspired many to become converts to the Nation of Islam. One of the most famous was a young boxer named Cassius Clay. The 22-year-old boxer, while training for a match in Miami against famed fighter Sonny Liston that would determine the heavyweight champion of the world, invited Malcolm X and his family to stay with him while he prepared for the match. Clay had been inspired by Malcolm X's depiction of his faith, and when Clay defeated reigning champion Liston in six rounds to become the new heavyweight champion, he publicly announced his conversion to Islam. At the same time, he announced that he was changing his name in keeping with his faith, taking a new name that had been given to him by Elijah Muhammad. In the future, he would be known as Muhammad Ali.

had the authority to order such an act: Elijah Muhammad. Malcolm X had become so popular in New York that the Messenger's rule there was being jeopardized.

With great anguish, Malcolm X ended his association with the Nation and looked for a new path to follow, although he had little doubt where it would lead. "My life," he said, "was inseparably committed to the American black man's struggle." No matter which direction he took to carry out his continuing quest for a revolution, he knew he would remain true to an earlier vow to "never forget that any wings I wore had been put on by the religion of Islam."

8

A Time for Martyrs

Malcolm X announced at a crowded press conference in March 1964 that he was leaving the Nation of Islam to found an organization called Muslim Mosque, Incorporated. It was to be centered in New York City, where a core group of about 50 participants—all former members of the Nation—would act as "the working base for an action program designed to eliminate the political oppression, the economic exploitation, and the social degradation suffered daily by twenty-two million Afro-Americans." He invited blacks of all religious denominations to join the group.

Without spelling out a specific agenda for his new organization, Malcolm X made it clear that Muslim Mosque was to be a revolutionary group. He stated that blacks should seize control of their communities and form armed resistance organizations to protect themselves. "Like Samson," he said, "I am ready to pull down the white man's temple, knowing full

In 1964, Malcolm X left the Nation of Islam after a falling out with Elijah Muhammad. He began to study orthodox Islam, and following a pilgrimage to Mecca, he adopted a new, more moderate philosophy and no longer based his beliefs on racist interpretations of Islam.

well that I will be destroyed by the falling rubble." He was willing, though, to make some uncharacteristic concessions. He was willing to join forces with less radical black leaders. Whites were also welcome to contribute money and ideas.

The news of Malcolm X's organization sent ripples of excitement through Harlem. The leaders of the Nation, however, were enraged and unleashed a savage attack on him. Muslim newspapers branded him a hypocrite and traitor. The

Nation's lawyers filed suit to reclaim title to Malcolm X's house, and the group's leaders even ordered his brothers Wilfred X and Philbert X to denounce "the traitor" publicly.

Malcolm X, though stung by this onslaught, responded calmly. "When you're involved in a revolution," he remarked, "nothing is painful." He set up his headquarters in Harlem's Theresa Hotel, where he preached the word of Allah and the gospel of political revolution, and he appeared at rallies, where he exhorted listeners to band together behind a unified militant movement and stand up to "the man," the ghetto term for whites. "You have to walk in with a hand grenade," he said, "and tell the man, 'Listen, you give us what we've got coming or nobody is going to get anything.'"

Malcolm X's split with the Nation freed him from its inflexible doctrines, and he widened his horizons. He developed an interest in orthodox Islam, as practiced in the Middle East, and he began studying with Mahmoud Youssef Shawarbi, an Egyptian professor working in New York. He learned from Shawarbi that in the Islamic faith people were judged by their actions, not their color.

Shawarbi also guided his pupil toward a careful study of Islam's holy book, the Koran, whose scriptures caused Malcolm X to question many of his old assumptions. Even before he had broken with the Nation, his conversations with Muslim students from North Africa and the Middle East—many of whom looked as "white" as any white American—had shaken his belief in the Nation's racial doctrines. These students did not quarrel with Malcolm X's political views, but they argued that his bitter denunciation of the white race did not square with Islamic teachings. Privately, he had begun to wonder if the students were right.

A PILGRIMAGE TO MECCA

Malcolm X's doubts about his own racial attitudes grew until he became deeply troubled. To help resolve his inner turmoil, he undertook an important mission: He went to Boston to visit his half-sister Ella, who had shocked him three years earlier by joining the Nation and then surprised him again by quitting the Nation and joining a more traditional Muslim group. Ella had stood by him throughout his trials, and now he had one more favor to ask of her: Would she lend him money for a pilgrimage to Mecca, the Islamic holy city?

All Muslims who are physically able are required to make at least one such pilgrimage, known as the hajj, to the holy city. Malcolm X's time had come at last, and Ella quickly agreed to sponsor his trip to the Saudi Arabian site. In April 1964, scarcely a month after announcing the formation of Muslim Mosque, Inc., he left quietly on his hajj. Only his wife and a few

IN HIS OWN WORDS...

Malcolm X's pilgrimage to Mecca transformed his views—and his life. In an open letter to the press, he revealed how his experience of sharing the hajj with an international, interracial group of fellow pilgrims had dramatically altered his understanding of Islam:

There were tens of thousands of pilgrims, from all over the world. They were of all colors, from blue-eyed blondes to black-skinned Africans. But we were all participating in the same ritual, displaying a spirit of unity and brotherhood that my experiences in America had led me to believe could never exist between the white and non-white. . . .

Each hour here in the Holy Land enables me to have greater spiritual insights into what is happening in America between black and white. The American Negro never can be blamed for his racial animosities—he is only reacting to four hundred years of the conscious racism of the American whites. But as racism leads America up the suicide path, I do believe, from the experiences that I have had with them, that the whites of the younger generation, in the colleges and universities, will see the handwriting on the walls and many of them will turn to the spiritual path of truth—the only way left to America to ward off the disaster that racism inevitably must lead to.

close aides knew where he was going. The pilgrimage was a personal matter he wanted kept out of the spotlight.

Mecca proved to be a revelation to Malcolm X. He marveled at the spirit of brotherhood and the sense of community in the holy city. He was greeted warmly by Muslims of every race and nationality on his visits to shrines and mosques and felt a strong kinship with them—not only with black Muslims from Africa but also with white-skinned, sandy-haired Eurasian pilgrims. The bitter differences between the races seemed to melt away under the warmth of shared religious faith.

Like all pilgrims, Malcolm X prayed in Mecca's Great Mosque and walked around the central symbol of Islam: the sacred black stone that is kept in the Kaaba. He also had a number of discussions with Islamic scholars and clergymen who wanted to know if any aspect of his pilgrimage had affected him. "The *brotherhood!*" he told them. "The people of all races, colors, from all over the world coming together as *one!* It has proved to me the power of the One God." (For additional information on the hajj and Islamic rituals, enter "hajj" into any search engine and browse the sites listed.)

Malcolm X expanded on the effects of his hajj in an open letter to the press. He wrote that he was "spellbound by the graciousness I see displayed all around me by people *of all colors.*" This "overwhelming spirit of true brotherhood" had prompted him to change his views on race and religion. "Despite my firm convictions," he said, "I have always been a man who tries to face facts, and to accept the reality of life as new experience and new knowledge unfolds it." In the future, he would judge people by their words and deeds, not by the color of their skin.

Malcolm X's main goal was still to organize black Americans for a revolt against white power and he was now willing to move swiftly and forcefully to the political center of the civil rights movement. He felt for the first time that, as he would later put it, "I can get along with white people who can get along with me."

Before leaving Mecca, Malcolm X celebrated his pilgrimage by taking an Islamic name, El-Hajj Malik El-Shabazz. He continued his spiritual journey by traveling to Lebanon and then to Africa, where many nations had recently gained their independence from European colonial powers. In Nigeria, students flocked to mass assemblies to hear the famed American activist speak, and they bestowed still another name on him: Alhadji Omowale Malcolm X. Omowale, which means "the child has come home" in the Nigerian language of Yoruba, was an apt name because he felt a strong bond with Africa. "I feel that I am at home," he told an audience in Ghana and added, "I'm from America, but I'm not an American."

Ghana's president, Kwame Nkrumah, entertained Malcolm X and then asked him to address the Ghanaian parliament. It was the ideal forum for Malcolm X. He had conceived of a broad new plan for linking the black African nations' struggle for political and economic independence with the struggle for justice waged by black Americans. He stated in his address that racism, poverty, and political oppression had common roots throughout the world, and that peoples of Third World nations—all of the underdeveloped countries on earth—must unite and guard against being economically exploited by powerful foreign nations and corporations. He called his new political philosophy "global black thinking."

The last stop on Malcolm X's journey was Algeria, which had recently won its independence from France. On May 19, 1964—his 39th birthday—he flew back to the United States. Much had changed in his brief absence. The country was in the throes of racial violence, even though civil rights groups had kicked off a new campaign with the hopeful phrase "Freedom Summer."

"Summer of Despair" was a more accurate term. In the South, black churches were firebombed, civil rights marchers were beaten by police, and the corpses of several activists were found in Mississippi fields. In the North, riots erupted in New York, Chicago, Philadelphia, and many smaller cities.

Malcolm X was prepared for this wave of racial disturbances. He drew up plans for a vast new movement that
would promote black consciousness throughout the world.
He met with a group of black radical thinkers and formed
the Organization of Afro-American Unity (OAAU), a non-
religious branch of Muslim Mosque, Inc. Its program included
traditional activist measures such as voter registration
drives and school boycotts along with community projects
aimed at improving urban housing and rehabilitating
drug addicts.

Malcolm X also envisioned the OAAU as a black nationalist
organization. Its agenda called for workers throughout the
world to unite for the purpose of dismantling the capitalist
economic system of private and corporate ownership of goods
and property, on which most Western nations rested. He thus
hoped to merge the black power movement with socialism, an
economic system in which goods and property are owned and
controlled by the state.

So grand a mission required large funds—something
Malcolm X sorely lacked—and he quickly set about raising
money. In June 1964, he embarked on a busy schedule of
speaking engagements and fund-raising rallies. He also
launched a lobbying campaign at the United Nations, which he
urged to pass a resolution condemning American racial policies.

In July, Malcolm X flew to Cairo, Egypt, where he addressed
a group of representatives of African nations at a conference
sponsored by the Organization of African Unity. The delegates
treated their guest as if he were an official American ambassador and listened intently to his words. "Our problems are
your problems," he told them. He then went on to argue that
the struggle of black Americans paralleled the efforts of the
emerging Third World nations.

After he gave his address, Malcolm X consulted with Islamic
clergymen for ideas about expanding his ministry in America.
He then took an extended tour of Africa. He was feted at

several receptions given by heads of state, including his long-time hero Jomo Kenyatta, president of Kenya.

Malcolm X returned to the United States in November 1964, only to learn that the OAAU had foundered during his five-month absence. He immediately began another round of speaking engagements, hiring the Audubon Ballroom and other dance halls in Harlem for his meetings. He worked at a tremendous pace, often going without sleep and hardly seeing his family. As always, his speeches called for a full-scale black revolt against whites. "We must make them see that we are the enemy," he said. "Let them turn the money for defense in our direction and either destroy us or cure the conditions that brought us to this point."

THREATS AND CHALLENGES

As the year drew to a close, Malcolm X began to fear for his safety. Several of his aides had already been attacked and beaten by members of the Nation of Islam. A carload of his followers had been assaulted in a Boston tunnel and had averted trouble only because one of Malcolm X's men had produced a shotgun. Matters worsened in December, when Malcolm X himself received a series of death threats at both his home and office. Suddenly, he felt surrounded by enemies. Both the Nation and federal agents kept him under close surveillance, and he suspected a conspiracy was being organized against his life.

Yet Malcolm X did not back down. Instead, he kept up his public speaking campaign. The riots of the Freedom Summer led him to believe that his radicalism might win new converts among the SNCC and other student protest groups.

In February 1965, Malcolm X went to London, where he addressed an organization of African nations. From there he proceeded to Paris, where he planned to speak at a rally protesting U.S. involvement in the Vietnam War. Soon after his arrival, the French government deported him on the grounds that he was a security threat, and he lashed out at French officials for calling his presence "undesirable." Then rumors reached him that officials had discovered a plot to kill him in Paris and had deported him because they wanted to avoid an international incident on their soil.

More danger awaited Malcolm X upon his return to New York, including an incident that brought back frightening memories of his early childhood. It happened on the night of February 13, 1965. He and his family were asleep in their home in East Elmhurst when gasoline firebombs crashed through the picture window in their living room. He managed to herd his family out of the house just before flames engulfed half the building.

All along, Malcolm X had been certain that these attacks were the work of the Nation of Islam: His vocal criticism of Elijah Muhammad and his followers was being met with vengeance. He now began to wonder. Some of the incidents, especially the alleged plot in France, seemed beyond the capabilities of the Nation. He suspected that white supremacist groups and perhaps even the FBI had joined forces and were bent on intimidating him into silence.

He would not let them succeed. In fact, his message would soon reach more people than ever before with the publication of *The Autobiography of Malcolm X*. For several years, he had been dictating the story of his life to writer Alex Haley, and the work was almost completed. Malcolm X hoped the book would clarify public perception of his views and goals.

On Sunday, February 21, 1965, Malcolm X and his aides drove to the Audubon Ballroom for his regular weekly meeting with the Harlem community. The hall was about three-quarters full when, at 2:00 P.M., he stepped onto the stage to begin the meeting. He faced the audience and uttered a traditional Muslim greeting, "*As-Salaam-Alaikum,* brothers and sisters!" At that moment a man in the front row stood up, pulled out a sawed-off shotgun from his coat, and fired a shot into Malcolm X's

Malcolm X was assassinated in 1965, at the Audubon Ballroom (seen here in the aftermath of the shooting), during his weekly meeting with the Harlem community. Although it was never confirmed, many suspected that the assassins were members of the Nation of Islam, upset by Malcolm X's challenge to Elijah Muhammad's authority and his disassociation from the organization.

chest. Two other men rushed forward and pumped more bullets into Malcolm X's body.

While the assailants fled the ballroom, Malcolm X's aides rushed to the side of their stricken leader. By the time he reached a hospital emergency room, the 39-year-old activist was dead.

One of Malcolm X's assassins, Talmadge Hayer, was captured outside the Audubon Ballroom, but his two accomplices—Norman Butler and Thomas Johnson—briefly escaped before being captured. The three were convicted of first-degree murder in March 1966. Police detectives suspected that the Nation was involved in the murder, but debate continues about precisely whether or not the three men had links to or were members of the Nation of Islam.

Some 1,500 people attended the funeral for Malcolm X, held in Harlem on February 27, 1965. After the funeral, friends took away the shovels from waiting gravediggers and instead buried Malcolm themselves, at the Ferncliff Cemetery in Hartsdale, New York. Later that year, his wife gave birth to their twin daughters.

THE LEGACY

As the 1960s wore on, other public figures, among them Martin Luther King, Jr., fell to assassins' bullets. Violence ravaged more cities. Malcolm X's vision lived on through all the turbulence, all the sorrow, and all the death. Although Muslim Mosque, Inc., dissolved shortly after his demise, other voices, including those of the Black Panther movement founded by Huey Newton and Bobby Searle, echoed his call for sweeping changes in American society. The Black Panthers seized on Malcolm X's phrase "the ballot or the bullet" and used it as their slogan. The Nation of Islam remained at the forefront of the black separatist movement, eventually forgiving Malcolm X for his supposed transgressions and once more embracing him as one of its own.

Today, Malcolm X remains the best-remembered black militant of the 20th century. There was a resurgence of interest in his life in 1992, when director Spike Lee released his film *Malcolm X*. Nation of Islam leader Louis Farrakhan cited Malcolm's accomplishments and sacrifice in his speech before hundreds of thousands gathered in Washington, D.C. for the Million Man March in October 1995, echoing the words of Malcolm X when he told the huge crowd that white supremacy was the root of America's suffering.

At Malcolm X's funeral, actor Ossie Davis noted that, although the activist would be remembered for his controversial words, his legacy extended beyond rhetoric: "Here—at this final hour, Harlem has come to bid farewell to one of its brightest hopes—extinguished now, and gone from us forever.

Betty Shabazz

Betty Shabazz is best known as the wife of Malcolm X, but her efforts on behalf of civil rights continued long after her husband's death.

Betty Shabazz was born Betty Sanders on May 28, 1936, in Detroit, Michigan. She studied at the Tuskegee Institute, a historically black college in Alabama, before moving to New York to work as a nurse. Friends invited her to attend lectures by Elijah Muhammad, and she soon joined the Nation of Islam. She met Malcolm X in 1956, and they married two years later. Within five years, the couple had four daughters.

When Malcolm X left the Nation of Islam in 1964, he and his wife took the Muslim surname Shabazz. Betty and their daughters were in the audience of the Audubon Ballroom in Harlem when Malcolm was assassinated in 1965. At the time, Shabazz was pregnant; later in the year, she gave birth to twin daughters.

Left with little money and a family of six to raise, Shabazz returned to college, first earning a B.A. in public health education from Jersey City State College and later a Ph.D. in education from the University of Massachusetts. She served as an administrator and later as an assistant professor at Medgar Evers College in Brooklyn and became a popular speaker, leading discussions on racial tolerance and civil rights.

In a 1994 speech, Shabazz voiced her suspicions (shared by others) that Nation of Islam leader Louis Farrakhan had been involved in the plot to assassinate her husband. A year later, her daughter Qubilah was arrested in Minneapolis, Minnesota, after attempting to hire a hit man to kill Farrakhan. Betty publicly supported her daughter, insisting that she was the victim of entrapment. Charges were dropped after Qubilah agreed to undergo treatment for alcohol abuse and psychiatric problems.

Shabazz later reconciled with Farrakhan, meeting with him during a fundraiser for her daughter's defense. In 1995, she spoke at the Million Man March Farrakhan organized in Washington, D.C.

Tragedy continued to haunt Shabazz and her family. On June 1, 1997, Betty was severely burned as a result of a fire in her home in Yonkers, New York. She lingered in critical condition for three weeks before dying. Shabazz's 12-year-old grandson, Malcolm Shabazz, Qubilah's son, was charged with setting the fire, reportedly because he was unhappy at being sent to live with his 61-year-old grandmother.

. . . Many will ask what Harlem finds to honor in this stormy, controversial and bold young captain—and we will smile. . . . We will answer and say unto them, 'Did you ever talk to Brother Malcolm? Did you ever really listen to him?. . . For if you did you would know him. And if you knew him you would know why we must honor him."

James Turner, the founding director of Africana Studies at Cornell University, experienced Malcolm X's passionate commitment to achieving true freedom for blacks. "This was a brother you could believe," Turner said. "There was the sense that he was not in it for something. That was the extraordinary thing about him. He was in it because of his commitment to our liberation."

At a time when Martin Luther King, Jr., was advocating peaceful resistance to achieve civil rights, Malcolm X's fiery arguments urging blacks to seize power through whatever means necessary represented a dramatic difference in the idea of how best to achieve social justice in America. Because Malcolm's positions moderated slightly near the end of his life, after his pilgrimage to Mecca, there is some thought that had both Malcolm X and Martin Luther King, Jr., lived longer, they might have discovered greater common ground in their views of the civil rights movement.

It is certain that Malcolm X placed a very different face on the struggle by people of color to achieve equality. It was often an angry face, a face that would not wait patiently for society to change but instead demanded respect and freedom *right now*. He spoke for a generation of young, politically active black people who felt betrayed by their country and, in some sense, by the slower pace of the civil rights movement.

Martin Luther King, Jr., understood this when he said, in a telegram to Betty Shabazz after her husband's assassination, "I always had a deep affection for Malcolm and felt that he had a great ability to put his finger on the existence and the root of the problem. He was an eloquent spokesman

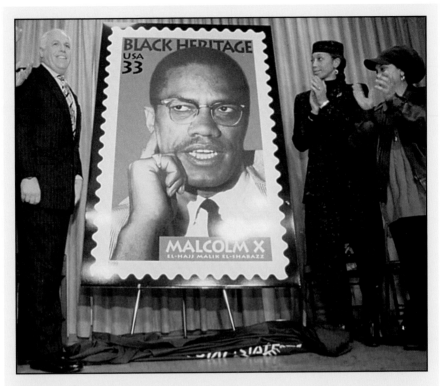

Though often radical and controversial, Malcolm X was a powerful spokesman who had a keen understanding of the issues of the black community. He is remembered today not only as a black militant, but also as a leader with a thirst for knowledge who was determined to bring justice to his community by any means necessary. Here, Malcolm X's daughter, Attilah, looks on at the dedication ceremony of the Malcolm X stamp in 1999.

for his point of view and no one can honestly doubt that Malcolm had a great concern for the problems we face as a race."

One of America's most compelling public speakers, Malcolm X would not let his fight for racial justice be stopped—not by his white opponents, not by his enemies in the Nation, not even by an assassin's bullet. His powerful example of black activism continues to be felt throughout the world.

1925 Malcolm X born under the name Malcolm Little in Omaha, Nebraska, on May 19

1931 Malcolm X's father is murdered

1942 Becomes a street hustler in New York City

1946 Sentenced to 10 years in prison for robbery

1948 Begins to educate himself while in prison

1949 Begins correspondence with Elijah Muhammad; converts to the Nation of Islam and changes name to Malcolm X

1952 Paroled from prison

1953 Appointed a minister for the Nation of Islam; organizes his first temple, in Boston, Massachusetts

1954 Appointed minister of Nation of Islam's temple in New York City

1958 Marries Betty X

1962 Appointed national minister of the Nation of Islam

1964 Breaks with Nation of Islam and founds Muslim Mosque, Incorporated; makes religious pilgrimage to the Middle East; founds Organization of Afro-American Unity; goes on speaking tour of Africa

1965 Assassinated in New York City on February 21

Adoff, Arnold. *Malcolm X.* New York: Crowell, 1972.

Breitman, George, Herman Porter, and Baxter Smith. *The Assassination of Malcolm X.* New York: Pathfinder Press, 1976.

Clarke, John Henrik, ed. *Malcolm X: The Man and His Times.* New York: Macmillan, 1967.

Du Bois, W.E.B. *The Souls of Black Folk.* Reprint of 1903 edition. New York: New American Library, 1969.

Essien-Udom, E. U. *Black Nationalism.* Chicago: University of Chicago Press, 1972.

Goldman, Peter. *The Death and Life of Malcolm X.* New York: Harper & Row, 1973.

Lincoln, C. Eric. *The Black Muslims in America.* Boston: Beacon, 1961.

Malcolm X. *Malcolm X Talks to Young Peop* ⸺: Pathfinder Press, 1965.

Malcolm X, and George Breitman, ed. *By Any Means ⸺ sary.* New York: Pathfinder Press, 1967.

Malcolm X, and Benjamin Goodman, ed. *The End of White World Supremacy.* New York: Merit, 1965.

Malcolm X, and Alex Haley. *The Autobiography of Malcolm X.* New York: Grove Press, 1965.

White, Florence M. *Malcolm X: Black and Proud.* Easton, MD: Garrard, 1975.

WEBSITES

Africans in America
www.pbs.org/wgbh/aia/

American Memory. The Library of Congress
www.memory.loc.gov/ammem/

American Rhetoric. Malcolm X
www.americanrhetoric.com/speeches/malcolmxballot.htm

The Civil Rights Coalition for the 21st Century
www.civilrights.org

Malcolm X: A Research Site
www.brothermalcolm.net

The Official Site of Malcolm X
www.cmgww.com/historic/malcolm/

ABOUT THE AUTHOR

Jack Rummel is a freelance writer who lives in Hoboken, New Jersey. He is also the author of *Langston Hughes* and *Muhammad Ali* in the BLACK AMERICANS OF ACHIEVEMENT series published by Chelsea House.

CONSULTING EDITOR, REVISED EDITION

Heather Lehr Wagner is a writer and editor. She is the author of 30 books exploring social and political issues and focusing on the lives of prominent Americans and has contributed to biographies of Frederick Douglass, Harriet Tubman, Sojourner Truth, Thurgood Marshall, Malcolm X, and Martin Luther King, Jr., in the BLACK AMERICANS OF ACHIEVEMENT, revised editions. She earned a BA in political science from Duke University and an MA in government from the College of William and Mary. She lives with her husband and family in Pennsylvania.

CONSULTING EDITOR, FIRST EDITION

Nathan Irvin Huggins was W.E.B. Du Bois Professor of History and Director of the W.E.B. Du Bois Institute for Afro-American Research at Harvard University. He previously taught at Columbia University. Professor Huggins was the author of numerous books, including *Black Odyssey: The Afro-American Ordeal in Slavery*, *The Harlem Renaissance*, and *Slave and Citizen: The Life of Frederick Douglass*. Nathan I. Huggins died in 1989.